John N. T. Helferich

Arms Export Controls under Siege of Globalisation

John N. T. Helferich

Arms Export Controls under Siege of Globalisation

Defeated Nation States or Voluntary Surrender?

Tectum Verlag

The Deutsche Nationalbibliothek lists this publication in the Deutsche Nationalbibliografie; detailed bibliographic data are available on the Internet at http://dnb.d-nb.de

ISBN 978-3-8288-4563-3 (Print)
978-3-8288-7618-7 (ePDF)

British Library Cataloguing-in-Publication Data
A catalogue record for this book is available from the British Library.

ISBN 978-3-8288-4563-3 (Print)
978-3-8288-7618-7 (ePDF)

Library of Congress Cataloging-in-Publication Data
Helferich, John N. T.
Arms Export Controls under Siege of Globalisation
Defeated Nation States or Voluntary Surrender?
112 pp.
Includes bibliographic references.

ISBN 978-3-8288-4563-3 (Print)
978-3-8288-7618-7 (ePDF)

1st edition 2020

Printed and bound in Germany.

Cover image: Typhoon at Cassele, Italy
Source: Eurofighter.com (2019) © Eurofighter – Geoffrey Lee

Inhalt

Preface VIII

Abstract IX

1.0 Introduction 1

2.0 Methodology 4

  2.1 Literature Review 6

3.0 Theoretical Foundations 7

PART I - Economic and Regulatory Developments 10

4.0 Liberalisation/ Privatisation in France, the UK and the US 10

  4.1 Liberalisation / Privatisation in Germany 11

  4.2 The Cold War Caesura 13

  4.3 The Organisation of the EU Defence Industry Today 15

5.0 Political Cooperation in Arms Export Questions 18

  5.1 Supraregional Control Bodies 18

  5.2 Common Regulatory Policies within the EU 22

  5.3 From Common Criteria to an EU Code of Conduct on Arms Exports 27

  5.4 COARM and the New Intergovernmentalism 33

6.0 Conclusions: Economic and Regulatory Developments 35

PART II - Transnational Production and National Controls 36

7.0 The German Export Control Regime 36

  7.1 The War Weapons Control Act 36

  7.2 The Foreign Trade and Payments Act (AWG) 38

  7.3 Principles for the Export of War Weapons and Other Military Equipment 38

  7.4 Regulatory Oversight over License Decisions 40

8.0 Legal Ambiguity 41

9.0 Export Control in Armament Cooperation 43

  9.1 The Eurofighter Typhoon 43

  9.2 Integrated Parts and Exemptions from End-Use Declarations 45

9.3 Application and Implementation of Guidelines 48
9.4 International Framework Agreements 49
9.5 Evaluation: Armament Cooperation 52
9.6 Theorising Armament Cooperation 53
10.0 Sub-licensing 54
10.1 Small Arms: Market and Perceptions 55
10.2 Government Stance and Policy 57
10.3 Restriction on the Delivery of Key Components 59
10.4 Legal Impediments 60
10.5 Post-Shipment Controls 61
10.6 Evaluation: License Production of Small Arms 63
10.7 Theorising License Production of Small Arms 64
11.0 Affiliated Companies and Joint Ventures 65
11.1 The Structure of the Rheinmetall Group 67
11.2 Rheinmetall Relations with the German Government 70
11.3 Government Stance and Policy 71
11.4 Technical Assistance and the Export of Data 71
11.5 Exerting Political Pressure 73
11.6 Evaluation: Affiliated Companies and Joint Ventures Abroad 75
11.7 Theorising Affiliated Companies and Joint Ventures Abroad 76
12.0 Conclusion and Outlook 77
13.0 Bibliography 79
Annex I: Interview Overview 91
Annex II: Practical example of Dual-Use licensing 92
Annex III: The EU Common Position Criteria 94
Annex IV: Glossary 95

Table of Figures

Figure 1: World military expenditure 1988 - 2017 6

Figure 2: Trend in transfers of major weapons 1979 - 2018 6

Figure 3: Global share of arms exports 2014 - 2018 13

Figure 4: Downsizing in the European defence industry, 1990 - 2001 14

Figure 5: European firms´ percentage of home vs international revenues 2013 17

Figure 6: US firms´ percentage of home vs international revenues 2013 17

Figure 7: Destination of EU Arms Exports 32

Figure 9: Diverted MG3 in Yemen 54

Figure 10: Sana'a school bus attack involving US MK 82 66

Figure 11: MK 83-bomb by RWM Italia found in Saada 66

Figure 12: MK 80 series General Purpose Bomb 68

Figure 13: RWM Italia share of MK 80 license revenues 68

Figure 14: Opening of SAMI Ammunition Factory 69

Preface

Today, the arms industry is increasingly internationalized, but arms export decisions remain a core prerogative of national governments. The question of whether and how the internationalization of defence production affects national arms export decisions is a crucial one.

To shed light on the different facets of this issue, John Helferich begins this work by contrasting the historical processes that led to the liberalization of the arms industry in Germany, on the one hand, with the emergence of international arms export control regimes on the other hand. Subsequently, the political dynamics that have influenced the common regulatory policies in the EU are analysed with particular reference to the implementation of the *EU Common Position on Arms Exports* as well as the *EC Dual-Use Regulation.*

Therein, a key finding is that the level of economic integration among multi-domestic defence companies trumps the level of political integration in arms export control questions in Europe. Moreover, it is found that the incomplete European export control architecture, entails economic disadvantages as well as a number of arms diversion risks. The latter Helferich conceptualises as phenomena of hyper-globalisation.

The body of the work is made up of three case-studies which focus on distinct scenarios where national export control practices face transnational trade contexts. Each of the cases reveal different empirical and theoretical insights on the matter. A broader conclusion that can be drawn is that despite the comparatively strict regularly stance on arms exports in Germany, the German government has only limited practical or political means to prevent the re-export of military goods once they have left the German jurisdiction. This is largely due to the high level of trade liberalisation that took place from the 1980s onwards and a result of particular foreign/security-policy choices that Germany took to re-establish its military-industrial base after World War II.

The work is based on interviews with 20 policy stakeholders in five countries and aims to bring practical export control procedures into a broader political and IR context. As such, the cases presented are examined through different theoretical lenses, arguing that arms export control policy is a multifaceted phenomenon demanding an analytically eclectic approach.

Based upon the findings of this study, a policy recommendation that Helferich puts forward is the need for standardisation of EU external exports as well as a deepening of cooperation in EU working groups, in particular COARM.

This study thus provides academic and policy-relavant insights on a topical debate.

Dr Hugo Meijer
Sciences Po, Center for International Studies, Paris
12 September 2020

Abstract

While defence industrial production and trade is increasingly transnationalised, the control of arms exports still takes place almost exclusively on a national level.

With the example of the German arms export control regime, this work seeks to analyse whether the current situation yields arms export control risks that could undermine German foreign and security policy principles. In a second step, inferences about International Relations theory are drawn based on the current regulation and its implementation.

Looking at three case studies in which national control regimes are confronted with transnational trade contexts, this work finds that transnational production and trade indeed creates a number of arms diversion risks, however, these risks are predominantly a result of deliberate political choices rather than a phenomenon of hyper-globalisation.

1.0 Introduction

Globalisation discourse has traditionally been separated into two camps that take opposite positions to the matter, but arrive at the same conclusion: on one side, those that argue that greedy market forces make it impossible for benevolent governments to protect their populations from the ravenous predators that lurk beyond their borders; and on the other side the ones that counter this view by arguing that benevolent market forces actually prevent greedy governments from fleecing their citizens (Wolf 2001, 1). Even though the two sides see different villains and different endings to the narrative, they draw one common conclusion: "omnipotent markets mean impotent politicians" (ibid.).

At first glance it appears difficult to situate the issue of arms export controls in this debate as the defence market is considered the most controlled and restricted market, in comparison to its civil counterparts. The underlying assumption is that it is good for a country that security matters are shielded from the commercial interests of other actors, be they states or members of civil society. Defence matters and armaments are generally seen at the heart of national security policy, therefore states´ monopoly of power over defence matters usually remains unquestioned. As a result, unlike in traditional markets for consumer goods, which are composed of a larger number of customers that industry can serve on its own initiative, demand and investment in the defence domain is almost entirely driven by governments. Moreover, due to the high level of costs and respectively risk associated with product development, the "prevailing worldwide model of product development for larger defence systems" entails that all of the research and development (R&D) costs are funded by governments (Commission 2016, 43). However, despite the fact that the defence market is more restricted than other economic areas, it appears to be a misconception to think that defence companies have little freedom to act independently and that defence trade has remained immune to globalisation.

In fact, the arms industry is increasingly internationally oriented as not only armaments projects but arms production itself become more and more transnationally organised (Markusen & Costigan 1999). This finds expression in the increase of international cooperation in armaments projects, a move towards the liberalisation of the defence industry as well as rising numbers of international mergers of defence companies. Especially in Europe, these phenomena are the results of decreased military spending after the end of the cold war, coupled with a constant increase in prices of military goods which forced governments as well as defence companies to cooperate across borders in order to remain competitive (Wolf 2015).

At the same time, while arms production and trade are becoming more and more transnationalised, arms export controls continue to take place exclusively on the national level. We might therefore face an imbalance between the "national scope of government and the transnational nature of markets" which Rodrik

(2011) calls the globalisation paradox (xvi)[1]. It appears that this situation is not only a challenge in the field of macroeconomic policy, taxation and income distribution, which are the usual focus areas of the globalisation debate, but that these challenges are also becoming more relevant in the defence and security field. Nonetheless, Rodrik (2011), Wolf (2001) and others assert that governments have an essential role in this narrative as the rules of the market were up to nation states to choose and thus governments could influence the depth and regulatory frame of globalisation. Markets need a wide range of non-market institutions in order to be politically sustained[2]. In economic terms this means that "the extent of the market is limited by the workable scope of its regulation" (Pearlstein 2011).

A dilemma that could arise is that the integration of the defence industry eventually trumps the level of political integration so that a state's capacity to freely decide over its arms exports declines. In Germany recent public debate was marked by a heated discussion over arms exports controls and the question of whether the current export control practices allow the German government to ensure that defence technology does not end up in the hands of undesirable end-users after it has left the country. For instance, in the context of the German elections in 2017, the use of German technology in attacks on civilians in Yemen has caused agitation and led the new government to ban exports to actors "directly involved in the Yemen conflict" (Coalition Treaty 2018, 149). However, a few months later, news sources revealed that German weapons are still being used in the conflict because of previously signed cooperation agreements and shipments from subsidiaries of German companies abroad (Grüll & Hoffman 2018).

These scandals raise the question whether the current legal framework and the way it is implemented allows the government to withstand market forces. Moreover, it raises the question of whether current German export practices really endorse a restrictive export policy or if these cases are deliberate foreign policy choices. Therefore, the following three case studies have been selected which present situations where national arms export controls are confronted with transnational production and trade contexts.

Cooperation - when two or more states, or companies from different states, decide to cooperate, it is necessary to strike a balance between export practices and the interests of the countries involved in the joint project. This may lead to situations where the export regime of one country is undermined by the partner country.

---

1 For Rodrik (2011) the paradox is that globalization will work for everyone only if all countries abide by the same set of rules enforced by some form of global government. In reality, however, most countries are unwilling to give up their sovereignty and their freedom to manage their economies in their own best interest.

2 The idea is that markets need an institutional context to exist as they are not self-creating/regulating/or legitimising.

Sub-licencing - when a foreign company purchases the rights to produce a product of a national company, the country in which the production occurs is responsible for authorising the final export of the good. In this case risks arise if the country of production ignores the consultation process and allows shipment to destinations that are against the security interests of the country who granted the license for production.

Affiliated Companies - as export control is carried out on a national level, it is possible for a company to move parts of their production to another country with laxer export regulations.

There are several reasons why this analysis will focus on Germany. Foremost, because the German export control regime is considered to be among the strictest in the world. Hence, if this research finds that the transnationalisation of arms trade has indeed created situations in which the German export control regime has been undermined, it is likely that these findings would also apply to other states with less stringent export controls. In addition, the German defence industry is marked by a higher level of liberalisation, compared to countries, such as France and Switzerland, in which governments still hold residual ownership rights over central defence companies.

As German firms are not directly managed by the German government they are able to act more freely on the global plain. The high level of liberalisation in the defence domain as well as German companies' global footprint engender manifold points of contact - and conflict - between national controls and the global defence market. Yet, comparisons to the legal frameworks of other countries, especially the United States, France and Switzerland will be made to provide comparative perspectives where necessary. Based on the previous analysis the research question is as follows:

Does the increasingly transnationally organized defence industry pose the risk that the foreign and security policy principles of the Federal Republic of Germany could be undermined by the uncontrolled proliferation of arms and armaments produced by German firms?

In doing so this work will:

1. Identify risks that can result from the trade of arms that is beyond the control of nation states, while at the same time showing areas in which concerns of hyper-globalisation are invalid.
2. Yield insights into the German arms exports regime and show potential shortcomings or exemplary practices.
3. Contribute to the discourse on the harmonisation of export policies in the EU

4. Provide insights into German foreign-policy based on the idea that arms exports are an intrinsic part of it.
5. Enlarge the discourse of IR theory by analysing the relationships between states through the lens of export controls.

Next, a section on methodology will clarify in what ways knowledge and data was acquired (Chapter 2-3). This work follows a mixed-method approach based on legal and foreign-policy analyses, which is complemented by qualitative interviews with policy stakeholders. The first part of the work serves to contrast major developments in defence production and trade with parallel trends in the control of military goods especially in Europe. Therefore, a historical analysis of defence industry integration and multilateral export control regimes is conducted (Chapter 4-6)[3]. The second part looks at specific cases in which transnational production challenges national export regimes. After outlining the major elements of German export controls (Chapter 7-8), the work transitions into an analysis of the three case studies: cooperation (Chapter 9), license production (Chapter 10) and affiliated companies (Chapter 11). Finally, the work concludes by highlighting the major findings regarding transnational export control risks and the theoretical inferences that can be derived from International Relations theory (Chapter 12).

2.0 Methodology

This work has a pragmatic as well as a critical orientation: the pragmatic goal is to shed light on the workable scope of arms export regulation in Germany in an effort to find out if it is fit for challenges related to globalisation; and the work is critical in that it aims to reflect on International Relations models based on the German arms export policy towards other states.

In operational terms, "hyper-globalisation in defence trade" shall be defined as the trade of defence goods and related services of nationally rooted companies against the intention of the government where the companies are rooted. Given the ongoing globalisation debate, particular attention will be paid to such `transnational´ forms of arms trade, for which "the borders of nation states are losing their influence and which lead to new demarcations and entanglements of and across nation states" (Wessler & Brüggemann 2012, 5).

As theoretical support, an eclectic mix of the different normative and philosophical traditions associated with policy analysis, International Relations and political economy provide the epistemological foundation for the research.

3 As Lequesne (2015) put it "history matters [..] to understand an international policy the scholar cannot limit himself/herself to what he/she observes empirically during his/her participatory observation or interviews" (14).

In terms of method, comparative public policy and case studies shall be employed to study the politics, political institutions, and foreign-policy conflicts associated with arms export controls. As such, a small number of cases will be compared within their real-world context in order "to better understand their qualities and to develop and investigate hypotheses, theories and concepts" (Hauge et al. 2016, 91). A special element of this approach is that comparisons will not only be drawn across countries, but also across history i.e. past and contemporary control frameworks and practices. The combination of the focused comparative approach with empirical inquiry has several benefits: Not only will it help to improve existing understandings and explanations of regulatory processes within the field of arms exports controls, but it should also reveal insights into the foreign-policy rationale behind national as well as multilateral export control arrangements. The analysis shall remain sensitive to the details of particular countries and their policies while retaining some ability to test existing theoretical propositions (ibid.) A variety of different sources have been used, including official government statements, as well as newspaper/ journal articles and documentaries relating to international arms trade and export control policy. The data sources that were accessed include national arms production and export statistics, the SIPRI databases, as well as transnational compilations such as the UN Register or EU impact assessments. Given that most of the important information in this field is not always public, interviews with policy stakeholders were chosen to complement the data set.

Therein, semi-structured interviews were conducted with five different groups of current and historical policy stakeholders: (*a*) civil servants in government departments and agencies (*b*) representatives of NGOs (*c*) scientists and (*d*) representatives from defence industry associations. Furthermore, officials in EU institutions and the German Embassy in Washington, DC supplemented this sample. The interview objectives were, first, to discover which legal provisions are currently (or still) in place and how they are implemented, second, to understand the functioning of multilateral consultation frameworks, third, to test attitudes of policy stakeholders towards transnational arms trade and export controls[4]. Interviews were by large carried out on a non-attributive basis.

In order to respect the anonymity of the interviewees, a code has been used in place of names (Annex I). This code is established by an abbreviation of the country where the interview was held, an abbreviation of the interviewees working area and a number to distinguish respondents that come from identical working

4 There are three main features of semi-structured interviews. First they take place with persons who are or have been involved in a particular experience. Second, they refer to situations that have been analysed prior to the interview. Third, questions are partially based on an interview guide that specifies topics related to the research hypothesis (Bryman 2016, 468ff).

areas and countries (e.g. GER-S-1). Overall, a total of 20 interviews were conducted in 2018; 22 interview requests were denied in large for reasons of secrecy of information. Due to the transnational nature of the research topic, interviews took place in different countries namely the USA (6), Germany (6), Belgium (6), UK and France (1 each).

2.1 Literature Review

There are a number of political developments that have led to an increase in the intensity of the arms export debate. First and foremost, the high number of armed conflicts in the world and related to that the rise in arms sales and the increase in military expenditure which is at its highest since the end of the cold war.

Figure 1: World military expenditure 1988 - 2017

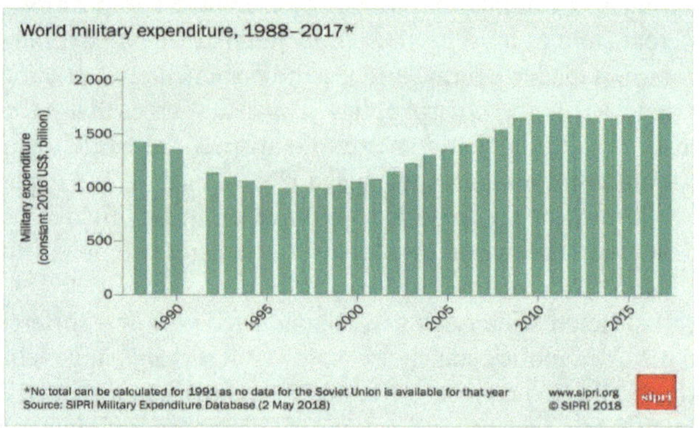

Source: SIPRI Military Expenditure Database (2019)

Figure 2: Trend in transfers of major weapons 1979 - 2018

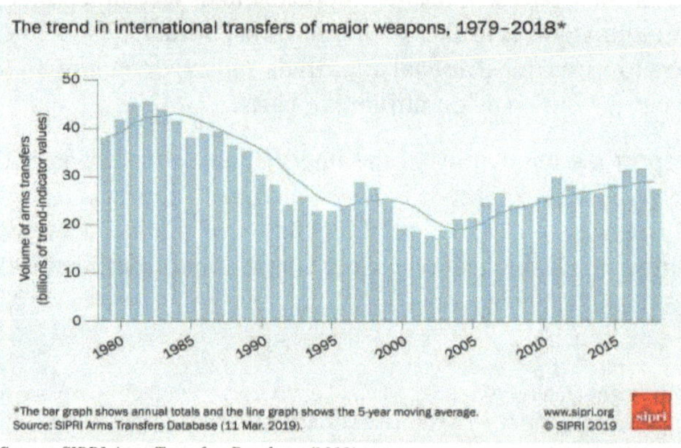

Source: SIPRI Arms Transfers Database (2019)

In addition to this, the introduction of the UN Arms Trade Treaty (ATT) in 2014 has intensified dialogue between civil society and governing representatives. However, much of this literature is politically motivated as it aims to provide policy advice, arguing either for more restrictive or for more industry friendly control practices. With regards to academic literature this work touches upon three related fields.

Firstly, there will be references to the globalisation of the political economy of the defence industry. This topic area has been looked at by scholars, such as Bitzinger (1994) analysing the increase in offset practices; James (2002) and Brooks (2005) examining the effects of foreign ownership on domestic weapons production; and DeVore (2013) looking at the effects of international cooperation on design, development and production of weapon systems. A second related field to this work is foreign-policy analysis in the context of arms production and trade. On this matter, there have been works by Béraud-Sudreau (2014) and Gabelnick & Rich (2000), focussing on historical analyses of defence trade or by Meijer (2016) looking at US foreign policy interests at the example of dual-use exports to China.

Yet, these works are often only peripherally concerned with arms export controls practices, which is the field that this work is most closely related with. As such, this thesis has benefited from previous efforts by Ian Davis´ (2002) comparison of the German, Swedish and British arms export control regimes. Due to the limited amount of literature, the author has sought to derive information from non-academic sources, for instance from trade journals that give practical advice to export practitioners, such as the German HADDEX and AW-Prax. With regards to data, the most renowned institution that works on international databases is the Stockholm International Peace Research Institute (SIPRI). In Germany, data about exports can be found in the Report on Military Equipment Export Control, which was introduced in 1999 and is issued annually by the Ministry for Economic Affairs and Energy (BMWI), and additionally the reports from the Joint Conference Church & Development (GKKE)[5].

3.0 Theoretical Foundations

In addition to the empiric/pragmatic element, this work also seeks to enlarge theoretical discourse by looking critically at what drives the implementation of export controls. The existing literature on IR theory applied to export controls shall serve as a mapping tool. Based on previous theoretical approaches to German

---

[5] The GKKE is an ecumenical association that seeks to increase the transparency in the field and support the adoption of an arms export control law that would aim for a legally binding restrictive export policy.

arms exports, (Platte & Leuffen 2016; Davis 2002) it is anticipated that decision-making takes place within the parameters of liberalism, political neo-realism and constructivism.

To begin with, liberalism's core assumption is that states are interdependent and rational and that collective interests are aggregated in institutional contexts. For instance, Germany, due to its size and economic power, is considered a major driver of European integration as it has promoted supranational policy-reforms such as the single market and the common currency at the expense of sovereignty. Arguably, these decisions were not purely based on a self-interested power-maximisation rationale, but on the belief that sharing power over certain policy domains is better for Europe as a whole. Specifically, in the context of European cooperation on export control one can expect decisions to bear traces of liberalist thinking.

Since the 1980s, the political concept of liberalism evolved into a particular economic philosophy that dominated the international economy, namely economic liberalism or neo-liberalism. It has formed the backbone of globalisation and brought to life ideas about international free trade, deregulation and fierce competition[6]. Davis (2002) argues that Germany and other major European states have increasingly adopted the logic of economic liberalism and "the global division of labour in their pursuit of prosperity" (22). On a neo-liberal reading, the national interest is primarily economic and this therefore trumps concerns about security or human rights (Platte & Leuffen 2016, 564). Furthermore, neo-liberalism as a theory of economic thought conceptualises arms as predominantly economic goods.

However, liberal thinking on the international economy has been countered by neo-realist thinking which has dominated the international political system for much longer[7]. Neorealism is grounded on the idea that states attempt to preserve or improve their power relative to other states in a self-interested manner. Yet they do so within a structured system of states which is defined by specific principles, such as anarchy and decentralisation. Within that system, the relative positions of states are thought to be a function of their technological and economic development (Nye 1988, 236). Put simply, countries with a strong military-industrial-technological base can exert power over states that do not have such capabilities. Evidence for that is that states consider export control as an intrinsic part of national sovereignty and that powerful states, such as the US can enforce arms exports regulations beyond the national border. This approach dominates the

---

6 Economic Liberalism as a theory of economic thought (not IR) has centrally shaped armament strategies and arms export policies in the 20th century.

7 Neo-realist theory initially was conceived as a theory of international politics and not of foreign policy. Nonetheless, neo-realism has increasingly been used for the analysis of foreign policy (Elman 1996, 8).

study of International Relations and it is likely to inform the policy making and implementation of export controls.

Finally, there is a further IR theoretical perspective – constructivism – which is at times left out of the equation as it is situated on a different spectrum (Wendt 1999). While positivist approaches such as liberalism and neo-realism assume that states are rational and utility maximising actors, reflectivist theories such as constructivism believes that actors are guided by a "logic of appropriateness" (Balsinger 2019, 1)[8]. Decisions that are taken based on "the logic of appropriateness" are biased toward "what social norms deem right, rather than what cost-benefit calculations consider best" (ibid). As a result, state behaviour is said to follow from the rules that govern the appropriate course of action for a given national role or identity. In the context of the negative experience of the two world wars, it is often argued that Germany's foreign policy is driven by ideational factors; notably its post-World War II identity. For that reason, scholars have referred to Germany as a civilian power which holds strong attachments to principles of non-military (but not pacifist), value-oriented multilateral foreign policies. Harnsich and Maull (2001) stress that civilian powers usually care strongly for the respect of human rights and therefore conduct a value-oriented foreign policy. Based on these assumptions, one can expect that constructivist ideas also play a role in certain arms export control decisions.

Davis (2002) has suggested that civilian powers with a flourishing defence industry face a dilemma nowadays. On the one hand they have to take on an active role in promoting exports in order to be able to keep unit costs to a minimum and maintain a profitable defence technological industrial base (DTIB). On the other hand, they must keep strong regulatory measures in place in order to (1) protect their security interests (2) ensure the technological superiority they enjoy (3) and fulfil the normative expectations of their citizens (22)[9]. These somewhat contradictory roles that states must fulfil form the background of the debate on transnational military production. While some authors have tried to subsume arms export decision-making under one of the International Relations paradigms, this work takes a more analytically eclectic approach by trying to qualify how each theoretical notion is reflected in the specific case studies in order to derive broader conclusions (Katzenstein 2010).

---

8 The logic of appropriateness is commonly distinguished from the logic of consequences. The latter assumes self-interested rational actors with fixed preferences and identities whose behaviour is determined by "the calculation of expected returns from alternative choices" (Balsinger 2019).

9 This dichotomy is also referred to as the "autarky-efficiency trade-off" (Moravcsik 1991).

PART I - Economic and Regulatory Developments

4.0 Liberalisation/ Privatisation in France, the UK and the US

The following section serves to illustrate the increasing integration of the European defence industry which runs parallel to the rise of international institutions and committees involved in questions on arms exports controls starting from the end of the cold war. Among economists it is widely agreed that the 1980s led to a new wave of globalisation and marked a caesura in the western macro-economic system. Notable markers of that were the decrease in trade barriers, rise in foreign direct investment (FDI) as well as the reduction of communication costs which led to a "death of distance"[10]. Economists such as Rodrik (2011) refer to this age as the beginning of "hyper-globalisation" – a normative term that is associated with the idea that globalisation has gone too far as it allows multinational companies to avoid the rules and regulations of nation states which poses a threat to any state's sovereignty (200). Since this work is concerned with the potential negative effects of globalisation on the sovereignty of nation states it makes sense to start the historical overview in this period.

In the 1980s neo-liberal politics especially in the UK and the US were in the process of reshaping global politics including the defence market. While the defence sector was among the least affected industries, a fact illustrated in that most international defence transactions continued to fall outside the remit of GATT and other frameworks that affect international commerce, the shift in ideology had a lasting effect on the political economy of the defence industry (Hansen 2016). The major consequence of market liberalisation and the increasingly dominant neo-liberal paradigm was the belief that competition and market forces let alone are more effective economic drivers than state regulation. As a result, a state's legitimacy in intervening in the defence sector decreased and cost-efficiency approaches in state procurement and industry strategy became stronger (Beraud-Sudreau 2014, 11).

This deregulatory pressure undermined the dominant realist thinking that the military industrial aspects of international security should not be left to market forces. Moreover, the change in paradigm had a liberalising effect on the defence market. The implications were especially strong in Romanic countries as well as the UK, where defence companies were public but with the state as the main shareholder. In the UK, the Conservative Government of 1979 to 1983 privatised several assets as well as its defence champion British Aerospace, and the nuclear

[10] In this period the global South and East industrialised and became the "factory of the global North"; economists therefore speak of a second wave of globalisation (Baldwin & Martin 1999, 2).

research company Amersham International[11]. From that point on state ownership should become the exception rather than the norm, clearly illustrated by Secretary of State for Energy, Nigel Lawson's statement from 1981: "no industry should remain under state ownership unless there is a positive overwhelming case for it doing so" (Rhodes et al 2014, 2).

Similarly, but slightly later the French State partially privatised several companies (CGE in 1987; Matra in 1988). An important side-effect to this was that defence companies had to develop civilian production capabilities, which in turn decreased the monopsonistic influence of the state, as industry was now less dependent on state procurement. Nonetheless, until today the British and French governments still hold "golden shares" in their central defence firms, which allows them to be directly involved in certain business decisions[12].

4.1 Liberalisation / Privatisation in Germany

In Germany, the practical implications of neo-liberal politics were less disruptive, as the defence industry was not concentrated in state-owned corporations. In fact, even in the Nazi period, arms production took place in mainly private companies, which were involved in state armament programmes but not state-owned[13]. When the occupied rest of Germany was banned from producing any kind of armaments in 1945, the few state-owned factories such as Volkswagen (VW) were dismantled or privatised and converted to civilian production. When rearmament began in the late 1950s, German defence contracts were awarded to the existing private companies Rheinmetall, Krauß-Maffei, Siemens, Krupp etc.

However, these private companies only received a share of armaments of varying proportions as a second mainstay, in addition to their civilian production. The goal was to create synergy effects as in the case of the German shipyards that were able to use research findings from military submarine projects (eliminating oil loss, lowering vibration and noise emission) for cruise ships and thus achieve a competitive advantage to their French and British counterparts (Ger-S-1). In the post-war period, there has never been a state-owned war shipyard like in France or the USA.

This means that today's strongest defence firms in Germany started out as civilian factories, whereas French and UK firms only developed a civilian leg as a result of neo-liberal politics in the late 20th century. The effect is that German companies have been more independent of the state for very many years, yet they were also under more competitive pressure as the political will to sustain defence

11 After 1983 the British shipbuilders faced the same destiny and so did Rolls Royce in 1991.

12 This influence ranges from selecting members of the governing boards of companies to deciding with whom business deals shall be concluded.

13 The section draws from email exchanges between the author and Prof. Dr. Hartmut Küchle (28 August 2018).

companies was stronger in the UK, France or the US (Küchle 2005). This is also illustrated by the fact that in Germany there are no companies that have the status of a "National Defence Champion" unlike in the UK or France, where companies such as British Aerospace, Thales or the Naval Group are not merely large organisations but they are also expected to "advance the interests of the nation" internationally. This was made possible by state policies that actively supported the merger of large defence suppliers into very large corporations which then reached a "critical size and became viable on their own" (Markowski & Wylie 2007, 31)[14]. National champion policy promotes economic nationalism domestically and seeks to build giant companies that are pre-eminent in the global competition (ibid.).

A large part of economic literature suggests that defence production in general can be operated more efficiently by private companies as, unlike state-owned companies where losses can be covered by the Ministry of Finance, private companies are under more competitive pressure to be innovative and efficient (Küchle 2005, 20). For instance, French tank construction at GIAT (now Nexter Systems) was highly inefficient and deficient and could not keep up with the smaller competition in Germany from Rheinmetall and Krauß-Maffei. Furthermore, while other European states had just begun to release their defence production from the strict oversight of the state, Germany had already taken defence market liberalisation further by privatising research and operative services in order to render the Bundeswehr more cost-efficient (Spiegel 1972, 3)[15]. Ministerial Director, Günther Bode concluded in his report on the state of the Bundeswehr in 1978 that "almost the entire future planning of weapon and communication systems for naval and aviation lies in the hands of private companies" (Bode 1978, 14). This would have been unheard of in neighbouring countries. However, this kind of industrial organisation is likely to be a very important factor in explaining why Germany was able to come 6th in export ranking of 1978, only two decades after the largely destroyed industry had taken up military production again (Grässlin 2013, 40). Furthermore, Germany has `defended´ its position of being among the top global arms exporters ever since.

---

14 Germany also provided aid to its defence companies so that if there were no civil orders, government contracts for armaments were provided in order to keep production running and maintain skilled workers. Yet, the prevailing policy in the defence domain was focussed on oligopolistic competition and the idea that competitive pressure internally will make companies more efficient and attractive on the international market.

15 Companies such as the Marine Technology Planning corporation took over strategic planning for the Bundeswehr, something that would have been politically impossible in countries that held on to state-ownership models (Spiegel 1972, ibid.).

Figure 3: Global share of arms exports 2014 - 2018

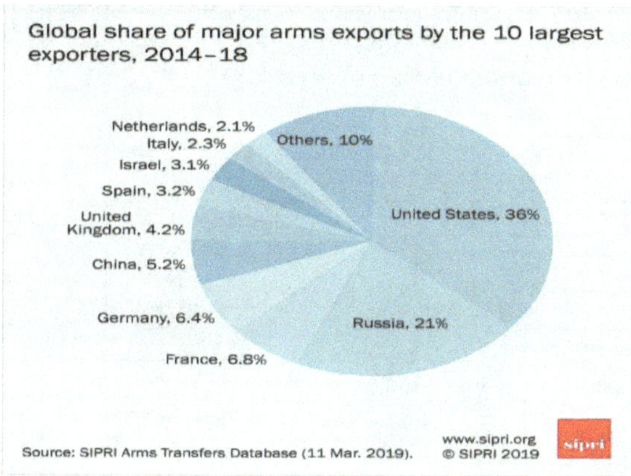

Source: SIPRI Arms Transfers Database (2019)

4.2 The Cold War Caesura

The end of the Cold War and the collapse of the Soviet Union marked a caesura in world politics. The move away from a bipolar world had implications for the security agendas of European countries, who were no longer caught in the middle of the two competing superpowers the USSR and the USA. Governments but also citizens more and more came to the realisation that excessive defence spending could also be used on welfare and civil investments – a concept that became known as the `peace dividend´ (Béraud-Sudreau 2014). This new mind-set undermined the arms industry, and in combination with the revelation of arms-related scandals in the context of the Gulf wars, there was increased activism of NGOs especially in Britain (Amnesty International; Oxfam) and in France (CCFD). These NGOs were created in the early 1990s and they strongly influenced the launch of a European-wide discourse on the introduction of human rights in the export decision-making process. Bromley et al. (2012) therefore write about the post-Cold War period that it "saw the introduction of human security principles into the field of arms export controls" (1035).

In addition, the new political and economic balance of power coupled with the decrease in military expenditure put pressure on the arms industry. In economic terms, the most immediate effect was significant cuts in defence budget and resulting from that, a reduction in jobs. For instance, the US defence budget dropped from \$422 billion in 1989 to \$290 billion in 1999 (Guay 2009, 88). In Europe, budget cuts were also very significant: 10% in France; 21% in the UK, and 29% in Germany. In fact, around 190 000 jobs were lost in the German defence sector between 1990 and 2001 – more than in any other EU country.

Küchle (2005) argues that the reason for the stronger recession in Germany is that private companies adapted to the reduction in demand to a greater extent than, for instance, the state-owned French companies due to governments′ interest in saving jobs in the sector (`Sarkonomics′) (Whyte 2007, 1)[16].

Figure 4: Downsizing in the European defence industry, 1990 - 2001

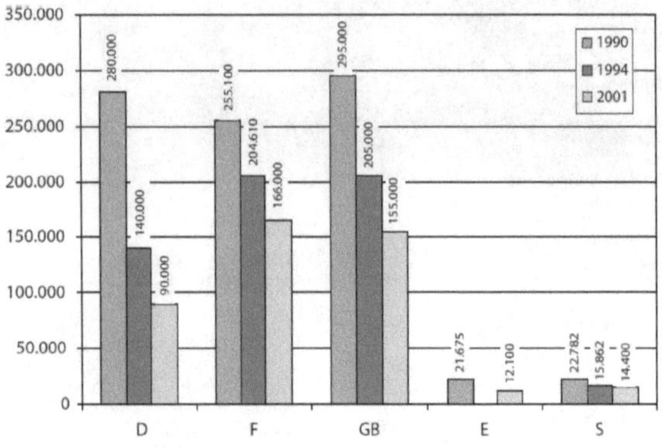

Source: Project Consult/ Syndex (2004)

Furthermore, not only did the internal demand decrease but the rest of the world were less keen on European weapons. This was partially due to the fact that the Soviet "going out of business sale" led to an uncontrolled spread of weapons on the black market. Even more importantly, new producers of weapons appeared in the global south and increased competition; most notably China, South Korea and Turkey. All of this led to a situation in which so-called "buyer states" were able to raise their demands in terms of offsets and technology transfers. The result was a contraction of the defence market to which Western defence companies hastened to adjust (Quéau 2013, 3).

This adjustment first started in the US between 1993 and 1998 where companies pursued strategies of downsizing and acquisitions in order to consolidate the defence industry[17]. In Europe, this consolidation process happened later and was less disruptive than in the US due to the significant political obstacles that hindered the process (Ger-S-2). Transnational collaborations existed almost exclusively in the form of multinational consortia or joint ventures for products like missiles (Guay 2009, 90). Both these factors enabled defence firms to maintain their national independence, which was also in the interest of politicians who were

16 Today, the defence industry accounts for 55 000 jobs in Germany, 140 000 in the UK and 165 000 in France (cf. Pauly & Steinmetz 2018).

17 In 2003, a Pentagon report found that the 50 largest defence suppliers of the early 1980s since had become the country's top five contractors (Schneider & Merle 2004, 1).

afraid that large scale-cross-border mergers could result in the loss of domestic defence companies.

By the early 2000s, this situation became unsustainable and given the consolidation in the US and the fact that other sectors had begun to take advantage of the Single Market programme (1993), European industry and governments found themselves under the political and economic pressure to consolidate (Guay 2009). High points of that period were the creation of companies such as Airbus (2000) or MBDA (2001). What followed was a range of political and economic decisions that revolutionised the European defence sector and can be seen as the starting point of the most recent stage in the history of a common European defence project which is marked by a move towards inter-operability of military equipment and independence from the US (B-EU-1).

4.3 The Organisation of the EU Defence Industry Today

Overall, the current state of the defence market in Europe has been described as a "spaghetti bowl" (Vlachos-Dengler 2004). This term refers to the post-consolidation ownership structure of the European armaments industry, with innumerable cross-shareholdings, segments and programme specific joint ventures, consortia and other legal arrangements (Meijer 2014, 59.) The question arises though if the restructuring of the defence industry has led to the creation of global defence giants which cannot be monitored or controlled – as Ann Markusen predicted it in 1999[18]. To answer that question, it is necessary to look at different ways companies can internationalise and apply it to the defence sector. Bellais and Jackson (2014) differentiate between three levels of internationalisation:

1. A firm can acquire other companies through merger and acquisition (M&A), only as part of an investment strategy, in a portfolio approach, but without any industrial dimension - similar to the investment activities of financial investors.
2. A deeper degree of internationalization would then also involve the "interpenetration of markets", for instance through the opening of production sites which serve to enlarge the sales of a given firm.
3. The third dimension concerns the reorganisation of production assets and research and development (R&D) capabilities across borders. The goal is to reduce excess capacities and to reach optimal production volumes on each site in order to be able to exploit economies of scale. This third stage may be considered "the culminating stage in internationalisation, which characterises globalisation in its specific nature" (238).

[18] Ann Markusen's (1999) work "The Rise of the World Weapons" is considered one of the foundational works in the discourse of hyper-globalization in the defence industry.

According to Bellais & Jackson (2014), defence companies have only reached the second step of internationalisation: they have opened production sites in different countries but without reorganising production assets. As a consequence, the internationalisation of such firms can be understood as an "extension of the domestic market as a result of the saturation of the original home market that is no longer large enough to allow firms to grow or even survive" (243). Nonetheless, semi-internationalisation or full internationalisation would not structurally change these firms as this stage requires a "deep consolidation of industrial assets" (Bellais & Jackson 2014, 234). Instead, the result of the large trans-border consolidations is the creation of "multi-domestic companies" (235). Such companies adapt their products to the local domestic environment but have largely independent production lines in different countries[19]. This view has been echoed by the European Commission in its Impact Assessment of the European Defence Fund (EDF) where the recent transformation of the European defence industry is deemed insufficient as it did not "reduce duplications and market fragmentation, nor did it allow the achievement of the full potential of cooperative programs" (Commission 2018, 13)[20].

However, even though restructuring has not led to fully globalised firms in an economic sense, defence companies today control more and more assets of companies in other countries than their home country. Once a firm has reached this dimension it is difficult to differentiate between domestic sales and exports (James 2002). This is because a firm can have several domestic markets for which it can produce independently and between which goods can be exchanged[21]. It would therefore be a misconception to think that multi-domestic firms are fully bound by the shackles of national restriction. This is especially the case for European countries which are decreasingly dependent on their home markets compared to for instance US firms.

19 In contrast, transnational companies sell identical products and have highly integrated supply chains.

20 Küchle (2018) notes that consolidation is hindered, inter alia by governments fear of (1) loss of sovereignty (2) national production sites, employment and know-how and (3) different export policies.

21 In 2011, BAE only generated one third of its revenues in the UK (£3.75 billion), whereas the remainder of the revenues came from abroad, especially the US (£7.29 billion). Similarly, Rheinmetall made 75% of its revenues outside Germany (Kollewe 2017; Rheinmetall Annual Report 2018).

Figure 5: European firms′ percentage of home vs international revenues 2013

Source: Frost & Sullivan (2014)

Figure 6: US firms′ percentage of home vs international revenues 2013

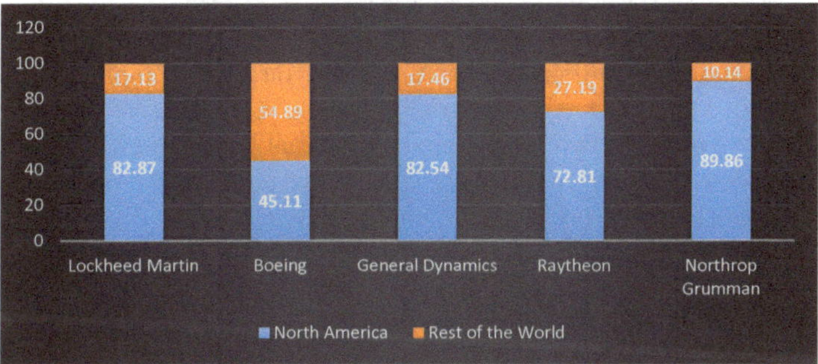

Source: Frost & Sullivan (2014)

Therefore, it is evident that the evolution of KNDS, BAE or EADS has transformed the relationship between firms and nation state. While the key founding firms - KMW, British Aerospace and Aerospatiale were controlled by one state and strongly dependent on its support, the new European giants have restructured and diversified in such a way that their industrial activities transcend national and regulatory frameworks. As Bellais and Jackson (2014) put it:

> Strategies of [...] internationalisation of defence assets have undermined the traditional state-firm relationship. Indeed, a reduced weight of domestic arms orders makes these firms less dependent on the defence policy of the state where the firm is headquartered and diversified arms markets can reduce the market power of a given state. Therefore, there is little to compel larger, more diversified and more international groups to follow

the guidelines fixed by, here, the British or French state rather than create a more autonomous strategy. One concern may be that arms-producing companies are then without governmental oversight and restrictions and therefore uncontrollable (236).

After having described the level of economic integration in the defence domain, the political frameworks that have accompanied this transformation shall be analysed.

5.0 Political Cooperation in Arms Export Questions

The first rigid national export controls were developed by major suppliers in the 1930s. These export controls were based around a conception of the national interest and as the foreign security and industrial interest differ greatly among states "there has been an almost complete absence of any universally agreed norms or principles governing the regulation of conventional arms transfers" (Davis 2002, 31). Most of the multilateral export control arrangements were created in the post-cold war period where the rationale for cooperation has been the non-proliferation of NBC weapons to states primarily located in the global south. However, major conventional weapon systems, dual-use equipment and small arms continued to carry fewer restrictions (F-S-1).

Today there are only two legally binding international frameworks: the denial of arms exports to countries which are under a mandatory UN arms embargo and the *European Common Position on Arms Exports*.

5.1 Supra-regional Control Bodies

In the following analysis of multilateral cooperation on arms exports control the focus will be on conventional weapons with particular reference to those agreements that affect the German export policy. The specific question that this section seeks to answer is to what extent multilateral control regimes have allowed Germany to remain informed about other countries´ exports of German armaments, and what means there are to stop exports that would undermine Germany's foreign and security policy[22].

---

22 This work is only peripherally concerned with NBC weapons. Yet, Nuclear weapons are covered by the 1968 Non-Proliferation Treaty (NPT) and the Nuclear Suppliers Group (NSG); chemical weapons by the 1993 Chemical Weapons Convention (CWC) and the Australia Group; biological weapons by the 1972 Biological and Toxin Weapons Convention (BTWC) and long-range missiles by the 1987 Missile Technology Control Regime (MTCR).

5.1.1 COCOM and Wassenaar

The German Federal Republic is a signatory of the Wassenaar Arrangement (WA), which means that it has translated its control principles into national law. The WA has its roots in the preceding *Coordinating Committee on Multilateral Export Controls* (COCOM). From the time COCOM was initiated in 1949 until its dissolution 1994, it provided the institutional context within which all NATO members (except Iceland) and a number of other countries managed their export control policies. The goal of COCOM was to introduce restrictions on the export of `sensitive´ technologies to communist countries in Eastern Europe, the former Soviet Union and Asia in order to "maintain a technological gap in the conception, design and development of military materials" (Alves 1992, 110). As COCOM was neither enshrined in a treaty nor was there a documented foundation for the committee, it operated on an informal basis.

The regime was centred around three lists that banned or limited the export of goods associated with nuclear energy, and goods and technologies associated with direct military use and dual-use[23] (Davis 2002, 33). Member States had to include these lists in their national export control regimes, which in effect resulted in partial trade embargos on prohibited countries. Exports of the more sensitive items by any member state required prior notification within COCOM, and proposed exports of the most sensitive items were subject to *veto* by any member (ibid.). This veto procedure was never repeated after COCOM dissolved in 1994, however, COCOM forms the basis of all subsequent international export control arrangements (Ger-S-1). With the end of the cold war, COCOM lost its purpose, yet members agreed to maintain the control lists through their national regulations until a successor regime would be established.

The successor regime came in December 1995, when representatives of 28 countries agreed to establish the *Wassenaar Arrangement (WA) on Export Controls for Conventional Arms and Dual-Use Goods and Technologies*.[24]. Wassenaar inherited COCOM's lists of dual-use and military items intended for use in conventional weapons. However, unlike COCOM, it has not embodied the veto-mechanism. Consequently, the decision to deny a transfer of any item is the sole responsibility of each participating state. As the WA is voluntary and nonbinding, it has no direct effect on national or international law as states are not legally bound to fulfil its terms and conditions in a particular manner. The WA has two lists. Firstly, the "Munitions List" for conventional arms which includes, among

23 The three lists were named: International-Atomic Energy List, Munitions List & Industrial List.

24 It was named after the town outside The Hague in the Netherlands where the preliminary agreement was reached but its meeting take place in a small secretariat in Vienna. The 42 participating states as at 6 Dec. 2018 are the 27 EU member states (except Iceland), as well as Argentina, Australia, Canada, India, Japan, Mexico, South Korea, South Africa, New Zealand, Norway, Russia, Switzerland, Turkey, Ukraine and the USA.

other goods, battle tanks, war ships and helicopters. For such goods members are expected to exchange information on deliveries to non-WA members every six months (Kimball 2017).

The second list is for "Dual Goods and Technologies" and it is divided into two tiers. The first tier, called "Basic Items", requires members to exchange information on all export licenses denied to non-WA members twice per year. Tier 2 refers to *sensitive items* and contains a subset for *very sensitive items* such as stealth technology or advanced radars. For those items members are requested to notify the Wassenaar Secretariat within 60 days, of (1) any export licenses denied to non-WA members, or (2) of export licences approved that are "essentially identical" to transactions that another WA-country denied within the past three years. This is to give other members time to persuade the exporting country to reverse the decision in security-relevant instances. However, this runs into problems as many exports happen before the 30 or 60-day deadline in which case the opportunity to consult is lost. In addition, members are not obligated to deny transfers previously denied by others, a process which is called `undercutting´ and which constitutes the major weakness of the regime[25].

The WA seems to be a useful but a modest approach to international oversight on conventional arms exports. Problems persist, foremost because members continue to be divided over its scope. Due to the fact that the WA operates by consensus, a single country can block any proposal. Especially at the beginning, several members consistently refused to fully participate in information exchanges and notifications on dual-use goods (Kimball 2017). In addition, there is no consensus among members on which countries are states of concern or what constitutes a "destabilizing transfer" (Joyner 2017). In 2004, the US Congress General Accounting Office (GAO) found that in only 36% of instances dual use consultations took place, and that members often take over a year to implement changes in their national systems (ibid.).

Given that globalisation has vastly increased the speed and volume of trade in goods and services, the WA appears to be unable to allow any individual state to influence decisions in time, especially if the other country involved in the process is not willing to share information or stop a certain transfer. Furthermore, even though the accession of India in 2017 brought new attention to the framework, some major arms exporters, such as Belarus, China, and Israel are not members. At this point there does not seem to be any intent to deepen the framework, as recent initiatives have been limited to updating the control lists in light of technological changes as well as the establishment of best practices recommendations[26].

25 The US has persistently urged members to give prior notification before granting an undercutting license, yet on Russia's demand no such rule has been put in place (Joyner 2017).

26 For example, mechanical high-speed cameras were deleted from the Control Lists as they have now been replaced by digital high-speed cameras in all sensitive applications.

5.1.2 The U.N. Arms Trade Treaty

The Arms Trade Treaty (ATT) entered into force on 24 December 2014 and was celebrated as a major paradigm shift in the regulation of the international arms trade. For the first time the global arms trade was – potentially – subject to international law. The ATT has thus far been signed by 135 countries and ratified by 100, including some of the world's biggest arms exporters such as the UK, France and Germany. Other major arms exporters, including the US and Israel, have signed the agreement, but not yet ratified it, while Russia, China, Israel, Turkey and 57 other countries have done neither. The ATT is in some ways a further development of the UN Register of Conventional Arms, yet in this case countries are obliged to report their transfers of the eight weapon categories mentioned in the UN Register[27].

What is even more important however is that the ATT also encompasses norms and principles that should guide the international transfer of conventional arms. The ATT is supposed to commit nations to stopping the export of conventional weapons if, as Amnesty International puts it "there is an overriding risk they could contribute to serious violations of international human rights or humanitarian law" (Amnesty 2017)[28]. The treaty also addresses previous issues of record keeping and reporting as in contrast to its predecessor, the UN Register of Conventional Arms, records shall include the quantity, value, model/type, arms actually transferred, details of exporting states, importing states, transit and trans-shipment states, and end users. Reports need to be submitted annually to the UN Secretariat but may exclude commercially sensitive or national security information. The goal is once more to improve transparency and information sharing, yet the institutional framework is weaker compared to the WA. For instance, Article 11 loosely stipulates that states shall take measures to prevent diversion and are "encouraged to share relevant information with one another on effectives measures to address diversion", yet no specific procedures are stipulated (6).

Five years after it entered into force it remains questionable whether the ATT's promise has been kept, as Amnesty has listed several examples of countries signing the treaty but then ignoring it. For instance, France, the UK, and Italy, who all ratified the ATT in April 2014, have carried on sending conventional weapons to Egypt while the Egyptian government continues to use brutal force against protesters (Amnesty 2017)[29]. This ties in with the issue of enforcement of rules and measurements to punish non-compliance. On this matter, members have again refrained from binding commitments. Article 14 - titled - "enforcement" - is limited

27 "Transfer" comprises export, import, transit, trans-shipment and brokering (ATT 2014, 4f).

28 Article 6: A state party shall not authorize any transfer of conventional arms if the transfer would violate arms embargoes, the Geneva conventions or international obligations related to illicit arms trafficking (ibid).

29 In 2017 only 54 reports - 61% of all members have issued reports and several of which were incomplete (https://thearmstradetreaty.org/).

to the phrase: "Each State Party shall take appropriate measures to enforce national laws and regulations that implement the provisions of this Treaty". Thus national law remains untouched, a result prompted by US arms lobbyists who feared that the ATT could affect the second amendment.

Furthermore, the introduction of the UN treaty did not have an effect on the volume of the international arms trade. In fact, the volume of international transfers of major arms between 2014–18 was 7.8 % higher than in 2009–13 and 23 % higher than in 2004–2008, according to the most recent data on arms transfers (SIPRI 2019)[30]. At the same, it is assumed that the actual effects of the ATT might only show in the longer term. Bromley (2017) stated that people are looking at the ATT through the lens of previous instruments such as the land mine treaty, which banned a whole class of weapons. That was never the aim of the ATT, instead "it was always about a much softer process of trying to create standards about the way states regulate the arms trade" (DW 2017, 3).

5.2 Common Regulatory Policies within the EU

The actual results of multilateral frameworks are difficult to measure, simply because states rarely publicise when or why an arms transfer was not authorised. Still judging by the number of violations of such arrangements, it appears that the major value of supra-regional oversight regimes lies in the steady harmonisation of exports control principles. However, as all agreements after the COCOM regime were limited to loose commitments of information sharing and could not directly influence national decisions (with no veto abilities), they had little power to prevent undercutting[31].

More potent approaches on conventional arms exports control have been made in regional arrangements especially in the context of the EU.

5.2.1 Exclusion of Military Goods from EU Competence

EU Member States have traditionally retained almost total sovereignty over defence policy matters, including arms export controls. This is based on Article 223[32] (a); (b) of the Treaty of Rome – now Article 346 of TFEU. Article 346 (a) states that Members are not obliged to disclose information "which it considers

30 In 2017, US firms increased their sales by 2% and now enjoy a global market share of 57%, Russian firms increased sales by 8.5% and hold 9.5% market share, German industry increased its sales by 10% and are responsible for 2.1% of global arms production.

31 This evaluation only refers to conventional arms export regimes, as it is commonly agreed that in the case of nuclear weapons, multilateral approaches have had a stabilising non-proliferation effect.

32 Article 36 also states that arms exports can be excluded from the implementation of the Treaty of Rome (TFEU 1957, 15).

contrary to the essential interests of its security" (TFEU 1957, 75). Moreover, Article 223 (b) allows Member States to exclude "the production of or trade in arms, munitions and war material" from Community competence where "it considers it necessary for the protection of the essential interests of its security" (ibid.). In order to determine which goods do not fall within the EU's remit, the Council of Ministers of the EEC, in 1958, was asked to "draw up a list of products"[33] to which the Article 223 derogation would apply; the list that was created was essentially a replica of the COCOM munitions list.

Technically, the existence of a list means that all other goods (i.e. non-Article 223 goods) should lie under EU responsibility. In practice, however, Member States have deviated significantly from this strict legal interpretation as they either apply exemptions to a wider range of products than those covered in the 1958 list or have interpreted Article 223 as if all areas covering national security were beyond the scope of the EU treaties (B-EU-1). This is of immense importance, because if export control was a supranational competence of the Commission, the interests of all Member States would have to be considered and not just predominantly those of the larger arms exporting states. This might have led to a higher level of transparency and a harmonisation of export controls right at the beginning of the European project.

5.2.2 Split of Dual-Use and Defence Related Goods

In the 1990s there was the growing realisation that economic convergence could only be achieved with a minimum of foreign policy coordination, which led member governments to review arms exports in the lead up to the Maastricht Treaty. At the time, several developments highlighted the inadequacy of the predominantly national approach to export controls within the EU. Firstly, during the Persian War much media attention focussed on the fact that weapons had been sold to both parties and moreover, that they were being used against their original producer (e.g. Operation Desert Storm)[34]. Secondly, the growing integration of Europe's arms industry created more permanent connections among companies, and the growing number of multinational corporations raised the question of how to control the movement of defence-related goods within such firms (Ger-S-1).

This was especially relevant because the impending establishment of the Single European Market (SEM) and respectively the free movement of goods threatened to undermine national controls as it raised the possibility that all goods that did not fall within Article 233 could be moved to, and exported from, the country with the weakest administrative or legislative system, if no further legislation was

33 The military products list was first published in 2001 and it is essentially the 1958 COCOM Munitions List. It was adopted by the Council of Ministers on 31 March 1958.

34 As a result of the destabilising transfers to Iraq, Germany tightened its national controls on dual-use transfers and pushed others to do the same (Davis 2002, 53).

passed (Davis 2002, 59). In order to allow for intra-EC trade but simultaneously ensure that security-related goods and technology did not leave the Union from countries with weaker controls to any `pariah´ state, it was necessary to decide (1) which goods could not be moved freely; (2) on which level the control of these goods (e.g. licensing, penalties for misconduct) would take place and (3) which common standards for effective external control would be established in order to avoid loopholes.

Even though it would not be necessary for controls at the external perimeter to be identical throughout the EU, "they would have to present a similar level of deterrence or a minimum standard at every point of exit" (ibid.). This put arms exports controls on the Maastricht agenda and many European political leaders believed that there might be a window of opportunity for the introduction of a common Regulation on this issue.

While Germany and the Netherlands were generally in accord with the view that EU export control policy needed to be extended to conventional weapons and should involve the drafting of specific criteria to establish a European framework for export licence decisions, they faced severe opposition by France and the UK who championed the opinion that these were questions of immense geopolitical importance that should not be imposed on Member States (F-S-1). In the end, the latter view was adopted and as a result a more pragmatic solution was sought. It was a compromise that left Article 223 and conventional arms untouched and only focussed on the harmonisation of technical and administrative procedures for dual-use goods (Davis 2002).

This is how dual-use goods were separated from military goods, which is still the case today. The solution left the external political dimension of conventional arms exports for future intergovernmental cooperation, and made dual-use goods a community competence, albeit with certain limitations.

5.2.3 The EC Dual Use-Regulation - Legal Provisions and Practical Impact

The EC-dual use regulation standardises the control of exports of dual-use items, including to some extent, software and services. It establishes a common list of goods for export outside the EU listed in Annex I and a list for intra-Community trade in Annex IV of the regulation. When it comes to intra-community trade, the majority of goods can be traded freely except for some particularly sensitive items which need to authorised prior to their transfer. The Regulation "transposes [...] the multilateral export control regime into EU law" which members must incorporate into their national export control regimes (Commission 2016, 21). The regulation is directly applicable throughout the EU[35]. However, enforcement and

[35] Since 2014, the European Commission can update the item lists through delegated acts in order to keep pace with economic and technological changes.

penalties are paradoxically managed on the national level. In practice the procedural terms are rather complicated and it is the responsibility of the exporting firm to ensure that it is complying with the export rules. An example that illustrates the complexity of the licensing procedure for Dual Use goods can be found in Annex II of this work. It outlines the different steps companies have to take to ensure they are fulfilling all the regulatory requirements.

Despite the complex regulatory framework and the variety of lists, and provisions that restrict dual-use trade, there have been significant pitfalls in the practical implementation of the Regulation. The first issue arises as a result of extreme differences in the interpretation and application of the regulation across Member States. In an EU survey, 60% of industry stated that the regulation gives rise to significant distortions between companies located in different Member States. Furthermore, 14 % declared that they have received a denial for a licence application when another exporter fulfilled the deal through an identical export from another Member State (Commission 2016, 6). This hinders intra-community trade as an exporter that is based in one country, and outsources certain parts of the production to another EU country may face different requirements for the export of the same good.

A side issue to this is that there are insufficient exchanges among licensing authorities. Because there is no obligation to inform other Member States on how the regulation and specifically the catch-all clause is implemented, licensing requirements differ. In the context of the deeply intertwined European industry, a lack of exchange between Member States can lead to undercutting and to so-called "licence shopping by dubious exporters seeking the most accommodating licensing conditions" (ibid.). Only since 2012 has an electronic system called DUeS existed which allows for the secure exchange of information between MS and the Commission, for example on denied exports. Yet, a joint study of SIPRI and Ecorys (2015) on behalf of the Commission found that the system is not used very frequently and that denial notifications often contain insufficient data to determine whether there is a match between items that were denied in one state and approved somewhere else (Commission 2015, 105). Thus far it seems that not enough synergies have been developed[36].

A second observation is that the system is highly complex and that the majority of the administrative burden is on the companies. This comes at a price, as the costs related to licensing and compliance are comparatively high. Based on licensing data, the overall yearly cost of licensing in the EU exceeds €100 million (Commission 2016, 12). This is especially problematic because licensing regimes of competitor countries are more cost-efficient and less complex. Research has shown that in the EU, 2.4% of exports require a license as compared to 1% under

36 For instance, a fully-shared IT infrastructure or a "catch-all database" that could be shared with customs and other enforcement agencies across the EU is still missing.

US regulation. This is further complicated by the fact that companies have insufficient knowledge of licensing requirements (ibid.). These obstacles create incentives for companies to move production outside the EU. Yet, this points to the problem that there is no level playing field between EU controls and those in third countries, especially the Middle East and Africa. Even though the EU has funded an "Outreach Programme on Dual-Use Export Controls" for third countries, there seems to be no real possibility to enforce end-use verification under the current framework[37].

The Commission (2016) finds that dubious exporters (state and non-state) take advantage of the complexity and vulnerability of integrated value chains, so that "proliferation risks move across borders and jurisdictions" (12f). For instance, proliferators have learnt to create sophisticated networks which employ foreign (non-EU) transport operators who are unfamiliar with proliferation risks. Especially given that the volume of dual-use goods continues to rise and more and more items are trans-shipped via third countries, this increases risks of diversion[38]. At this point, it appears that the EU lacks a constructive export control dialogue that would allow for end-user verification programmes or mutual recognition of internal compliance programmes with non-EU countries.

A third observation relates to the controls of services and intangible technology. Such immaterial transfers cannot be controlled by usual customs practices. The current list-based regime applies controls on the export of items from the EU customs territory but neither addresses intangible technology transfers nor the risk of circumvention by EU persons in third countries. As exports are increasingly "transmitted, not transported", online trading platforms are transforming the nature of supply chains and making it possible for anyone, anywhere, to act as a middleman or broker in a dual-use export transaction (Commission 2015, 88). This requires a clearer and more harmonised definition of the term "exporter", which at the moment is implemented in various ways across the EU and not well-adapted to prevent illicit brokering services[39]. Therefore, the Commission has suggested a revision of the EU jurisdiction clause so that EU persons located in Third Countries can be penalised as well.

To conclude, under the current framework, it is possible that a German company that is internationally organised within the EU, ships a dual-use good to a Member State with a laxer implementation of the regulation in order to increase

37 The 2013-2014 programme supported outreach to 28 countries, with a budget of €3 million.

38 For instance, EU exports to major trans-shipment hubs, such as the UAE increased by 130% from 2004 to 2014, at a time when they were at significant risk to be diverted to e.g. Iran and North Korea (Stewart & Gillard 2015).

39 Specific licensing for brokering services was introduced in the 2009 amendment, but is not implemented by many MS, including Germany. The basic principle underlying EU brokering is that such services are not controlled systematically but only when there is a clear risk of WMD or military end-use.

the chances of receiving an export license. Arguably, this is more difficult for very sensitive goods as chances increase that it is listed in Annex IV of the regulation. Once the good has left the EU though, the lack of dialogue with other countries, coupled with the specific nature of dual-use goods make it extremely difficult to ensure that trade of dual-use goods and related services does not undermine the foreign-security policy of Germany.

5.3 From Common Criteria to an EU Code of Conduct on Arms Exports

While the trade of dual-use goods does not always have an impact on human security, the trade of conventional weapons arguably does. The foundation of today's *Common Position on Arms Exports* lies in the eight *Common Export Criteria* that were agreed in 1991 again in the context of the Maastricht Treaty. They were the first notable advance towards a common European arms export control policy as they emphasised that decisions on arms exports should take account of the internal and regional situation of recipients, as well as their human rights record. In the context of the establishment of the Common Criteria a group of experts from each country was formed to examine issues related to conventional arms exports.

The purpose of the *Ad Hoc Working Group on Conventional Arms Exports* (COARM) was to compare national legislation and explore possibilities for further action. Today it is still the central forum for intergovernmental exchanges on arms exports in the EU (B-COARM-1). However, the Common Criteria had no effect on national sovereignty whatsoever and did not erase any differences in military product lists for the basis of granting export licences. In essence, the criteria were merely a statement of intent and "it is doubtful whether they made any significant difference to the arms export behaviour of Member States" (Davis 2002, 245)[40]. As a result, COARM was asked to examine this problem and consider what measures would be necessary to formalise the Common Criteria into a politically binding EU Code. Under pressure of the European Parliament and several NGOs, COARM produced a draft that was rather restrictive and focussed on human rights and development (Cops et al 2014, 40). However, EU foreign ministers adopted a watered-down version as France threatened to jeopardise the entire agreement, if a restrictive Code was chosen (Ger-S-2).

Eventually, on 8 June 1998, the *EU Code of Conduct on Arms Exports* was adopted as a legally non-binding Council declaration. It applied to legal transfers of all types of weapons - light and heavy, small and large. The guiding principles

40 Numerous examples illustrate diverging export policies in the 1990s: In 1994 the German go vernment refused to agree a warship contract with Taiwan, while France supplied Mirage fighters and frigates worth an estimated $6.2 billion. Portugal imposed a unilateral arms embargo because of Indonesia's invasion of East Timor, while Germany and the UK continued to supply warships and aircrafts (Eavis & Shannon 1994, 5; Davis 2002).

of the Common Criteria were integrated into the Code and further elaborated. Furthermore, the Code provided for information exchange and consultation. The Code's significance lied in the denial notification mechanism and the associated "no undercutting without consultation" which is very similar to the WA procedure. Yet again, there was no veto procedure which meant that after the consultation period the export may be authorised. In that case, however, the exporting country had to provide a detailed explanation of its decision. The operation of the Code was strengthened by two further developments. Firstly, in the course of the first annual review of the Code, a Common List of Military Equipment was adopted in June 2000.

It is based on the WA Munitions List and acts as a reference point for Member States when deciding which items should be subject to controls. Secondly, since 2003, COARM has begun publishing a regularly updated User's Guide for the interpretation of the eight Common Criteria[41].

5.3.1 From a Political Code to a Legal Common Position

The Code of Conduct merely constituted a political commitment, meaning that members were politically bound to conduct their export control in the spirit of the Code, but they were not legally forced to implement and enforce it under national law. The review of the document began in 2004 but it was not until 2008 that sufficient political momentum existed to take the Code to the next level. In fact, it was mainly political pressure from the European Parliament that allowed to turn the Code of Conduct into a (more) legally binding Common Position.

In 2008, the European Commission launched the European Defence Package, which was set out to Europeanise the tendering politics in the area of defence procurement. This was done via Directive 2009/81/EC which aimed to increase cross-border access to the procurement of defence goods plus related works and services[42]. The second part of the defence package was Directive 2009/43 which aimed to reform the internal market for the trade in defence-related products. In essence, the latter directive decreased the administrative burden associated with intra-EU defence trade by exempting certain transfers from licensing requirements[43]. It was warmly welcomed by arms exporting Member States, however,

---

41 MS were also obligated to submit an annual report on the export of military Equipment. Since 1999 these national annual reports have been merged into a consolidated EU report that is public.

42 As the call for tenders and other procurement activities is usually organised on an almost exclusively national basis, the Commission has sought to increase competition in the defence market by getting MS to open such calls to applicants across the EU.

43 Most notably, products that are not on the EU common military list shall not be controlled by MS when traded within the common market; transfers to armed forces or government bodies shall be exempted; fewer restrictions on the transfer of components and a shift towards general licences that and ex-post authorization.

due to the co-decision procedure, it required the support of the EU Parliament, which used the defence package as `bargaining power´ to obtain agreement on the conversion of the politically binding Code of Conduct into a legally binding Common Position (Cops et al 2017, 40)[44].

The Code was replaced by the *Council Common Position* 2008/944/CFSP in December 2008. It advocated a strong discourse of restraint, stating that "Member States are determined to set high common standards which shall be regarded as the minimum for the management of, and restraint in, transfers of military technology and equipment" (Council 2008). The criteria of the Common Position 2008/944 (without sub-clauses) are listed in the Annex of this work.

Even though the EU Common Position was not expected to revolutionise the way arms are traded by EU Member States, it did provide new elements that were, however, very similar to the provisions of the previous Code. Yet, for the first time the range of activities that should be covered by member states' arms export licensing systems were formally captured. In this regard, Article 1 states that arms export licensing systems should not only cover physical exports but also licensed production, brokering, transit or transhipment licences and "any intangible transfers of software and technology" (Council 2008, 2).

A certain hierarchy was put in place by requiring member states to *deny* an export licence if the transfer was deemed to conflict with any of criteria 1–4, but only to *take into account* the factors listed in criteria 5–8 when considering a licence application. A new central element is Article 5, which requires a reliable end-use declaration by the recipient country for the issue of an export regulation. EU Member States are supposed to verify the use of manufactured products and to consider the risk that products may end up in the hands of undesirable end-users when transferring production facilities for military equipment[45].

Nevertheless, all in all the differences between the Common Criteria of 1991 and those in the Common Position from 2008 are rather limited, and consequently, arms exports from the EU have been evaluated against almost the same criteria for the last 30 years. Moreover, the assertion of the "legally binding character" claimed by the Common Position and its related instruments (user guide, mutual consultations and the database for rejected export applications) is not in line with the general understanding of a "sanction-bearing legal force" (Moltman 2012, 13). Under Article 29 of the Treaty of the European Union (TEU), Member States are

44 Hansen (2016) argues that the adoption of the CP was possible because France no longer saw an agreement on lifting the embargo on China as a necessary condition prior to consenting to the CP anymore, partly because domestic developments in China had made lifting the embargo impossible (208).

45 Further relevant articles are related to: the obligation to report on an annual basis which exports have been authorised and how the Common Position has been implemented (Article 8); to adhere to the user's guide (Article 13) and to review the document after three years (Article 15).

obliged to adapt their own national export rules in accordance with the guidelines of the Common Position, yet, how this is done in each case is not specified. As a result, national governments still autonomously determine the extent to which these principles are integrated into national legislation and how the criteria are interpreted. The enforceability of the principles remains very limited though because a Common Position is a legal instrument within the Common Foreign and Security Policy (CFSP) and thus the European Court of Justice has no formal authority.

Similar to the introduction of the ATT, the Common Position led to inaccurate expectations by NGOs and other parts of civil society. It was believed that updating the Code of Conduct into something more binding aimed at posing barriers to risky arms exports. However, the document does not conceal that the limitation of arms transfers was never its intention[46]. Rather, in many parts of the document, one can merely identify the concern to make arms export policy compatible with the CFSP.

Therefore, the Common Position of 2008 is more to be a vehicle that seeks to prove that a coordinated external behaviour by the EU and its Member States is possible. Despite this, it is formulated in a way that provides significant room for interpretation.

5.3.2 Inconsistencies in the Implementation of the Common Position

Several Studies have assessed whether the EU initiatives, specifically the Common Position has led to increased convergence and harmonisation in arms export policy. A rather comprehensive analysis was conducted by the Flemish Peace Institute (2017) which scrutinised the national context, legislation, policy and public debates on arms export controls in eight Member States[47]. In none of the categories the study found complete EU wide-harmonisation but instead varying levels of convergence. The study found that while the implementation of the EU Common Military List has significantly harmonised the material scope of EU Member States' arms export control systems, important differences remain. This is because Member States' interpretations of the concept of "goods especially designed for

46 According to the 19th annual report, the number of denied licences fell in total and in relative terms (only 0.76% of licence applications were denied in 2016 compared to almost 1% in 2015).The criteria invoked for denials differed in their application, with criterion 1 being invoked 82 times, criterion 2 119 times, criterion 3, 103 times, criterion 4, 85 times, criterion 5, 8 times, criterion 6, 12 times, criterion 7, 139 times, and criterion 8, once (cf. Parliament Report on the Council's 19th Annual Report 2018, 8).

47 The study compares the implementation of the Common Position as well as the Defence Package in Belgium, Germany, France, Hungary, Netherlands, Portugal, UK and Sweden.

military use" diverge significantly due to differences in foreign and security policy priorities This leads to a situation in which different goods are being subjected to different licensing requirements (Cops et al. 2017, 188).

Furthermore, governments also continue to have diverging policies on assessing and controlling the end-use of defence-related goods through *re-export restrictions*. This is especially significant for transfers or exports of components where "domestic sensitivities and priorities result in diverging forms of national implementation of the Common Criteria" (ibid.). Even though almost every member States has implemented the Common Position in some way or another the Common Position is implemented in different administrative policy domains, because the institutional embeddedness of the arms export controls differ across Member States.

Germany, for instance, chose a rather soft solution: it simply annexed the document to its *Political Principles for the Export of War Weapons and Other Military Equipment*. The Political Principles, however, are merely an administrative guideline for civil servants but do not constitute an enforceable legal basis by which politicians are bound. In other words, the Federal Security Council, the highest executive organ for arms export decisions is not bound by the Common Position. That is why there are more and more voices in the Bundestag calling for the Common Position to be anchored in German law. This should make the Criteria generally applicable to all export decisions and not only to "discretionary decisions" (Moltman 2012, 14). In the current system the Common Position merely provides a point of orientation, but it is not a maxim that guides every export decision.

Reports by BICC and the *GKKE* analyse whether the German export decisions comply with the Common Position, considering factors such as the human rights situation, domestic stability and the compatibility of arms imports with the development prospects of the recipient country[48]. According to the most recent report, in 2016, the German Government granted 4,658 licences for the export of military equipment to 85 states, which can be classified as problematic with regard to *at least one* of the eight criteria of the EU Code of Conduct. Furthermore, in 2016, arms exports were approved to 45 countries that did not meet *at least four* of the criteria. In the view of the GKKE this shows complete disregard of the principles of the Common Position. Similarly, the European Parliament stated it was "alarmed by the fact that 97.2% of licence requests for exports to Egypt and Saudi Arabia were granted even though exports into both countries violate at least criteria 1 to 6 of the Common Position" (EU Parliament 2018, 7). Bearing in mind

48 As data basis for the evaluation of individual countries BICC uses various sources, including the World Bank's periodic reports, Amnesty International's human rights reports, and the World Military Expenditure Data of SIPRI.

that failure to meet criteria 1 to 4 must lead to a denial of the licence, this high number is a rather significant indicator for the document's ineffectiveness[49].

Figure 7: Destination of EU Arms Exports

Source: EU Parliamentary Research Service Blog (2015)

Despite these vital shortcomings, there has been a large consensus among NGOs and political elites that the Common Criteria have increased transparency. Since the sixth EU annual report from 2004, Member States have been asked to present data on the financial value of both actual arms exports and export licences, subdivided by destination and the 22 categories of the EU Common Military List (Bromley 2012, 7). This information is published in the EU annual report together with aggregated data on licence denials. Further improvements in the amount of information shared include the addition of tables showing the number of consultations initiated by each EU Member State, the number of consultations carried out for each destination country, as well as on granted and denied brokering licences. The Common Position has not only created a political obligation to collect and report data but it also led to more detailed reporting which made states more aware of transparency levels in other member states (ibid.).

However, in recent years there have been signs that transparency is in decline, as members gradually delayed the submission of the relevant information. The last two reports have been a blow to transparency as both the 18th annual report for 2015 and the 19th report for 2016 were published two years late[50]. Also, no significant progress has been made on the introduction of a more standardised

49 Parliament (2018) "regrets" that 95% of licenses for exports of vessels of war (listed on ML91) to Saudi Arabia have been granted even though they were later used to enforce the naval blockade on Yemen, "contributing to the deterioration of the humanitarian situation and to the ongoing suffering of the population of Yemen" (7).

50 The EU Parliament is therefore calling for the introduction of a strict deadline for submitting data of no longer than January following the year in which the exports took place (Parliament 2018).

submission and reporting system, which means that a number of Member States still do not make full submissions[51].

The Parliament concluded that as a result of the missing data, the COARM annual Report "is not up to date or able to present a complete picture of Member States′ export activities" (EU Parliament 2018, 7). Finally, the introduction of the Common Position has neither led to a reliable harmonisation of export controls that would ensure the German government that national companies operating in another EU state face the same level of controls when exporting military equipment as in Germany, nor do the transparency measures that were put in place allow the identification and control of export activities of German firms in other EU countries.

Yet, given the tradition of secrecy in that policy domain, it does not come as a surprise that the public documents are insufficient to allow governments or civil society to be informed about a certain export in another country so that they could oppose it or even hold politicians accountable. The question remains though, whether exchanges on individual exports happen formally or informally in closed EU fora, such as in the context of the COARM working group.

5.4 COARM and the New Intergovernmentalism

The Common Position can be seen as an expression of the `New Intergovernmentalism′ that has evolved in the EU in the Post Maastricht era. The term is used by different authors in slightly varying contexts but in short it can be defined as an approach to European integration that aims to achieve top-level policy coordination based on intergovernmental deliberation and political self-commitment of Member States, rather than through legislative decision-making that would reinforce the community method by transferring competences to supranational institutions (Bickerton et al 2015; Puetter 2012). The Common Position is exemplary for this kind of policy-making which is demonstrated by the fact that the consultation procedure remained untouched since the 1998 Code of Conduct, and because any discourse on giving up sovereignty in that field is vehemently denied by Member States.

Consequently, the method practised remains the same as in other policy areas, namely, to discuss differences in `closed shops′ - in this case the monthly COARM working group meetings. Interviews with a former EEAS chairperson of COARM have shown though that the nature of these deliberations is collaborative and hardly ever gets confrontational as disagreements are dealt with bilaterally (B-COARM-1). This is due in part to the fact that many armament contracts

[51] For instance, Greece did not submit a report, Cyprus submitted a "nil-report", Italy and France only reported total data on the value of actual exports and Belgium, Germany, Ireland, Malta and the UK did not report financial values of actual exports (ibid.).

are established on a bilateral basis and often involve Memoranda of Understanding (MoU) that clarify the ways in which countries shall consult each other when conflicts on exports arise. Therefore, individual license decisions would not be discussed under COARM unless they are of a significant volume and already part of the public discourse. Part of the reason why open discussions and the consequent necessity to justify oneself is avoided in the circle of the EU states is because such procedures would affect the national sovereignty of the individual state (ibid.).

Unlike in COCOM where national sovereignty was deemed less important than individual license decisions, which manifested itself in the veto-mechanism, the COARM meeting show a different hierarchy of interests. Several interviews have pointed to the fact that `confidence building´ among allies, which was central in the initiation of COCOM, is only a secondary purpose of the COARM meetings due to the geographical proximity of EU countries and the tightly interweaved European industry (B-COARM-1). Therefore, the focus of the working group lies on "long-term rapprochement between proponents and opponents of exports to third-country destinations" (Moltman 2012, 32). Furthermore, the aim of COARM is more practical, that is to jointly reflect on the security situation in a given recipient country (ibid.).

To illustrate this, in mid-2018, exports to Indonesia were in the focus, as some countries were rethinking their export policy in the context of rising corruption and human rights violations. In this case there would be a "tour de table" during which each member explains how they handle exports to the country of concern (B-COARM-1). While some states voiced concerns about weapon sales to Indonesian police, others doubted the government's credibility when it came to fulfilling re-export accords and a third group expressed confidence in the country's military and suggested that naval and aviation products could be sent without further ado (ibid.). However, individual license decisions regarding specific products or companies were not discussed, nor would a member criticise the export practices of another state openly. This dynamism is especially interesting given that the vast majority of COARM members do not export arms and could therefore call for more transparency or take a stricter stance on the seven exporting countries. This again reveals insights into the balance of power between core and periphery in these working groups.

The attempt to provide a political counterbalance to the interests of the exporting countries is hindered by the fact that the European Parliament cannot, or only to a limited extent, exercise its supervisory functions in the area of the CFSP because nation states assert their prerogatives in this field. When asked whether the Common Position is effective, Governments generally answer in the positive and only voice critique over the implementation of the user guide (B-EU-1). Yet, any veritable means to ensure convergence in the application of the User Guide, for instance, through the introduction of a peer-review process to mutually evaluate decisions, justifications and procedures of others, has not been part of the discourse.

At present there is no formal instrument to assess how and with what binding force individual states implement the Common Position, nor is there a possibility to intervene or sanction in case of non-compliance (B-EU-1). Moreover, given that Member States do not even share information on individual positive decisions and completed transfers, any enforcement procedure seems unlikely.

6.0 Conclusions: Economic and Regulatory Developments

The discussion of the internationalisation of industry in contrast to the evolution of multilateral supply regimes yields a number of conclusions. On the industrial side, multi-domestic defence companies have not transnationalised in all areas of production, however, they can nevertheless be described as transnational, as their strategies and ownership levels transcend traditional national-political boundaries. This is illustrated by the fact that such companies are decreasingly dependent on the original home market as they operate in different states and have leeway when it comes to deciding which markets to access, where to settle and where to export from.

On the political side, transparency and mutual consultations have generally increased, yet control measures have changed very little over the last 30 years. This is because Member States pursued harmonisation via intergovernmental approaches, motivated by neo-realist thinking which deems national sovereignty over export decisions superior to collaborative decision-making. In addition, all multilateral supply regimes discussed contain significant loopholes in their implementation. In practice there seems to be an absence of universally agreed norms or principles for exports of conventional arms, except for commonly agreed arms embargos. All of this creates several risks of unintended diversion or what can be described as hyper-globalisation in defence trade. Especially the study of the regulation of Dual use goods in the EU has shown that transnational companies can circumvent stricter national export controls by shipping a good to an EU country with laxer controls before transferring it outside of the EU. This is mainly because the deregulation of dual-use trade in the EU was not accompanied by a standardisation of controls for external trade. In other words, hyper-globalization happens when defence industrial integration and market deregulation exceeds the degree of political integration in export controls.

In the following section, the German export control regime's ability to influence transnational trade and production shall be discussed with the above findings informing and complementing this discussion.

PART II - Transnational Production and National Controls

7.0 The German Export Control Regime

In Germany, the principal legislation is made up of three legal texts that regulate who is responsible and how arms exports shall be handled. The Constitution of the FRG and more specifically Article 26 (2), stipulates that "weapons designed for warfare may be manufactured, transported or marketed only with the permission of the Federal Government. Details shall be regulated by a federal law".

However, in 1961 under Minister of Defence, Franz Josef Strauß, two laws were created (instead of one) to regulate arms and dual use exports: the War Weapons Control Act (KWKG) and the Foreign Trade and Payments Act (AWG). While the former takes a rather restrictive stance by stating that no-one enjoys an entitlement to the granting of an export licence for weapons of war, the latter is more openly formulated as it stipulates that foreign trade and investment of military equipment (not weapons of war) is generally not subject to restrictions.

7.1 The War Weapons Control Act

The War Weapons Control Act (KWKG) from 20 April 1961 regulates the export of all "war weapons" (NBC and conventional weapons) and some special components. The goods are defined by a War Weapons List (Kriegswaffenliste) that is divided into two parts. Part A covers weaponry that Germany has refrained from manufacturing, such as nuclear, chemical and biological weapons; part B covers all conventional weapons[52]. According to Article 1 §2 of the KWKG the government is entitled (in agreement with the Bundesrat) to amend the War Weapons List according to the latest scientific, technical and military knowledge.

In general, every export of war weapons requires a licence by the Federal Government. Moreover, "the export of war weapons is not licensed unless special foreign or security policy interests argue in favour of a licence in an individual case" (BMWI 2018). A license is required for the transport of weapons of war, if these goods are exported, in addition to the export licence. Therefore, two licences are required for exports of weapons of war in Germany, which is one of several elements that render the German export regime stricter than that of many other European Countries (Cops et al 2017, 90). The KWKG determines three sets of circumstances under which the export of weapons of war is to be prohibited §6 (3):

- if there is a danger that the weapons of war will be used in an act disrupting peace, in particular in an offensive war,

52 Part B covers items such as aircrafts, warships, combat vehicles, anti-tank weapons, mortars etc.

– if there is reason to believe that the granting of the licence would violate Germany's obligations under international law,
– if there is reason to believe that the responsible persons lack the necessary reliability.

If an arms export licence is denied the burden of proof is on the applicant to show that the refusal is unjustified, in court if necessary. It is important to note though that the clauses that prohibit an export, in practice, are secondary to the idea that exports can be licensed when "special foreign or security policy interests argue in favour of a licence". This leaves room for interpretation and according to interviews with former export control officials from the Ministry of Foreign Affairs, a foreign policy interest is already given when a foreign government wants to buy a certain armament. This is because the completion of the deal would have a positive impact on Germany's foreign relations, while a denial could potentially undermine Germany's interest in having close ties with this country (US-FO-1).

The example given was the sale of weapons of war and ammunitions to the Middle East, specifically Saudi Arabia. The country is among the top buyer countries for German military equipment, yet exports to Saudi Arabia have repeatedly sparked controversy due to the human rights situation, coupled with the war in Yemen, and most recently the murder of Jamal Khashoggi which eventually led to an export stop. Before the embargo, the export of goods listed on the War Weapons List could be justified firstly, because the government has an interest in maintaining good foreign relations with the country and secondly, because it is in Germany's security interest that Saudi Arabia is able to defend its territorial integrity especially in the context of the tense security situation with Iran. This did not mean that any listed good would receive an export license, but those that were unlikely to be used against the Saudi population, for instance patrol boats, were sent in large quantities[53].

The application of the clause in such a way makes it possible to export listed war weapons to conflict areas, which from a legal point of view is correct and according to the interviewee, not a violation of the principle that arms exports shall be handled restrictively with consideration to the human rights and economic situation in a country (US-FO-1). It is worth mentioning though that such exports are heavily negotiated between different government agencies and only authorised after the intended use of the item has been more or less `safely´ determined.

53 Patrol Boats are said to be unproblematic in terms of human rights violations as they are generally not used to beat down protests. In Germany this idea was coined by former Foreign Minister Hans Genscher who said "what floats goes, what rolls does not go". However, at least since the Saudis blocked Port Hudaydah which caused a humanitarian crisis in Yemen this idea has been challenged. Yet, it did not lead to a change of policy as the newly formed German government authorised the sale of patrol boats to Saudi Arabia in the 2018 coalition treaty. Only with the recent embargo the deal has been put on hold.

7.2 The Foreign Trade and Payments Act (AWG)

The *Foreign Trade and Payments Act (AWG)* regulates the trade of all goods, services, capital and other assets with foreign countries. The implementation of the AWG is outlined in the *Foreign Trade and Payments Ordinance (AWV)* which includes an export list with goods that require a licence before they can be exported. It is subdivided into three parts. Conventional weapons are listed in Part 1 A, which is essentially the EU Military list for arms exports and includes all weapons that are listed under the KWKG as described above. Part 1 B are specific nationally registered dual-use goods and part 1 C is made up of the EU dual use list. According to the AWG, foreign trade and investment is not generally subject to restrictions. For this reason, the applicant is basically entitled to receive an export licence unless essential security or foreign policy interests of the Federal Republic of Germany argue against it[54].

A licence can only be refused if Germany's security interests are endangered, the peaceful co-existence of nations is disrupted, or a substantial disturbance to Germany's foreign relations is likely (§ 4). It is important to note, however, that the government has a lot less power to prohibit the trade of "other military equipment" than the trade of "weapons of war". While the export of weapons of war is considered a privilege, the export of other armaments is considered a right, which means that the government has the burden to prove that one of the above reasons applies and a prohibition is legally justifiable in court. This is especially difficult when a company can refer to a precedent application that has received authorisation in the past. As a Foreign Ministry Official put it "when a company has built up a trustful relationship with a buyer over time, the government cannot simply deny an export for which there is a precedent by simply saying that our attitude towards this country has changed. There must be evidence that will stand up in court" (US-FO-2).

7.3 Principles for the Export of War Weapons and Other Military Equipment

The guidelines for the licensing authorities are further specified in the Policy Principles of the Government of the Federal Republic of Germany for the Export of War Weapons and Other Military Equipment. The Political Principles were born out of dispute between the SPD/FDP Coalition government in 1971. While Minster of Defence, Helmut Schmidt (SPD) advocated a complete ban on arms ex-

54 § 8 AWG "[…] The licence must be issued if it is to be expected that the undertaking of the legal transaction or action will not endanger the purpose of the provision or will do so only to a minor degree. In other cases, the licence can be issued if the national economic interest in the undertaking of the legal transaction or action will outweigh the related damage to the purpose cited in the authorisation".

ports outside NATO, Foreign Minister Walter Scheel suggested using arms exports and military assistance selectively as foreign policy instruments (Davis 2002, 169).

The compromise that was reached came in the form of the Political Principles, which introduced a differentiation between recipient countries. According to the most recent revision of the document from the year 2000, exports to EU Member States, NATO countries and NATO equivalent countries shall not be restricted, while exports to "Other States" are to be handled restrictively unless in specific cases where "this is exceptionally warranted on particular foreign/security policy grounds, having due regard to alliance interests" (Political Principles 2000, 4)[55].

The guidelines establish a number of other relevant principles. Firstly, that the government desires "to pursue a restrictive policy on arms exports" that takes into account the human rights situation in the recipient country as a key factor for the granting of a licence. Secondly, with regards to cooperation, that the government has "a special interest in the ability to cooperate" but that any new cooperation agreement to be concluded shall allow the government to assert its objections to a given export from the partner country. And thirdly, that war weapons and other military equipment may only be re-exported (or transferred within the EU) with the written agreement of the Federal Government.

Finally, the EU common Position is attached to the document which shall guide any export decision (ibid.). As mentioned above, the Political Principles are merely an internal bureaucratic guideline by which export authorities and the respective civil servants are bound in their daily work. Yet, ministers and executive bodies may disregard the guideline once a license decision has been forwarded to them. In other words, the power to enforce the principles lies with the politicians in charge of the relevant government departments, who are not however legally bound to adhere to the policy principles themselves.

Until now, calls for more parliamentary involvement in defence exports, for example through consultations on controversial decisions with the Bundestag have been denied. In 2014 the Federal Constitutional Court rejected the parliament's right to information in a law suit initiated by the Green party[56].

---

55 Australia, New Zealand, and Japan are considered NATO equivalent countries (Political Principles 2000, 2).

56 The court recognised that questions from deputies must be answered when it comes to the type and number of weapons as well as the total volume of the contract. However, anything beyond that, such as who was involved or the reasons for approval or rejection may be concealed by the executive organ. Presently, extensive or sensitive approved licence applications have to be reported to parliament within two weeks of the licence being issued (Hipp 2014).

7.4 Regulatory Oversight over License Decisions

In principle, German arms export decisions are embedded in a highly legalised framework where the licensing procedure depends of the nature of the products concerned. For weapons of war, the Ministry of Economic Affairs and Energy is the licensing authority in consultation with the Ministries of Defence and Foreign Affairs. In practice, most companies that intend to export a certain item listed in the KWKG, first make an inquiry before engaging in detailed negotiations with the interested buyer in order to avoid wasting resources on deals that are unlikely to be authorised (US-F-2). Such inquiries are managed by a handful of civil servants of the Ministry of Foreign Affairs, who then make an informal and non-binding decision on whether the intended export would go through. This evaluation is a reliable indicator on whether to proceed with the negotiations or not.

Once the company is ready to strike the deal, it submits a formal license request to the Ministry for Economic Affairs and Energy, which will then reach out to a number of departments in order to take a decision. First and foremost, the Ministry of Foreign affairs and the Ministry of Defence will be consulted in order to receive an opinion on whether such a deal could potentially violate the foreign and security interests of the government (B-EU-1). At the same time, the intelligence services will be tasked with finding out whether the final destination and the intended use are reliable or if there is reason for concern.

What is important, in this regard, is that the different Ministries often have different objectives and interests. In short, the Ministry of Economics is evaluated based on financial success as well as the number of exports, whereas the Foreign Ministry is concerned with maintaining good foreign relations. This can lead to situations in which two parties voice opposing opinions on an export in which case the dossier is delegated to the Federal Security Council (BSR). This is the highest executive organ in that policy domain and chaired by the chancellor[57]. The BSR is called into action if there is no agreement among the various ministries concerned and for "the most sensitive applications" depending on the nature of the product, the size of the order or the country of destination. Its meetings are usually prepared by the State Secretaries of the different ministries which submit drafts with their opinion on particular cases. The BSR then takes a binding decision. Yet the preparatory meetings and the council deliberations are shrouded in secrecy and not publicised.

For "other weaponry", *The Federal Office for Economic Affairs and Export Controls* (BAFA) is the licensing authority. BAFA based in Eschborn, near Frankfurt is a superior federal authority subordinated to the Ministry of Economic Affairs. It is responsible for the implementation of the *Foreign Trade and Payments*

57 Also, the Ministers of Defence, Economic Affairs, Foreign Affairs, the Interior, Finance, Justice, and Economic Cooperation and Development form part of the Council. For all BSR decisions between 2002 and 2014 (cf. Federal Government 2015).

Act which means that it issues the vast majority of licences. BAFA works closely together with the customs and intelligence agencies in an effort to prevent illicit trade. It is involved in a number of other activities, for instance hosting export control seminars and conducting end-use controls. End-Use controls are especially tricky when it comes to Dual Use Exports, which an official described as "detective work" (US-BW-2). As almost any good can have dual use character, depending on what it is used for, it is not enough to rely solely on the dual-use lists of the AWV. During interviews it was stated that BAFA sought for advice on the export of construction cranes, baby food and even female lingerie, which gives insights into the depth of dual-use controls (US-FO-1).

If there are grounds for suspicion, intelligence services or the embassy in the given country will be consulted in order to investigate the case. If the technical and legal review of the licence request results in the export not being subject to licensing, BAFA can issue a so-called 'Zero Notice'. It is a legally binding document which states that the export is neither prohibited nor subject to licensing. This means that the particular export is authorised but that it does not set a precedent for future export requests and that the exported good will not be added to any of the export lists.

In general, the vast majority of applications are routinely approved by BAFA on this basis. Only non-routine cases (less than 15%) are referred to the Ministry of Economics for consultation with the Foreign Ministry (ibid.).

8.0 Legal Ambiguity

Before analysing which loopholes may result from transnationalisation of production and trade, the issues associated with the current framework on the national level shall be outlined. NGOs have criticised the creation of two laws as not only a violation of the constitution, but as creating legal ambiguity. The rationale for creating two laws after WWII was economic and political. On the one hand, Germany was forced to take a restrictive stance on the trade of certain weapons as there were still constitutional restrictions put in place by the allied powers after WWII. On the other hand, the destroyed country had an interest in rebuilding its technological-industrial base and therefore sought to promote the export of all goods on which there were no restrictions (Ger-NGO-2). This decision still affects Germany today. The unique double structure creates ample room for interpretations and opens somewhat arbitrary categories of what constitutes a sensitive "weapon of war", in contrast to supposedly less sensitive "other weaponry". It is often particularly difficult to assign the requested export good unambiguously.

The War Weapons list only applies to a small group of central arms components for "weapons intended directly for warfare" (War Weapons Control Act

§1)[58]. However, this does not include other goods that are equally central to the function of weapons, such as radar systems, night vision equipment, fire control systems and the corresponding know-how. These goods, their components, and the corresponding services, are covered by the AWG and therefore companies are generally entitled to receive export licences for them. Applicants therefore have an interest in having the exported good "downgraded" so that it is no longer covered by the stricter KWKG, but by the AWG, which envisages the refusal of an export licence only in justified exceptional cases (Nassauer 2016). This option is particularly suitable for armoured vehicles and helicopters because exporters can transfer these items in two or more instalments. First the vehicle is sent in its civil-use form, followed by equipment parts such as attachments for machine guns.

Another example is provided by the export of drive systems for military vehicles. Engines and components used in propulsion technology for land systems are only covered if they are "specially designed for military use". The AWG formulation "specially designed for military use" means that the designer has designed the product solely or substantially for armament purposes and that the product possesses specific military functional characteristics (Monreal & Runte 2000, 144)[59]. This is not the case with many engines used for military land and sea vehicles - therefore these engines are not subject to licensing. As long as engine manufacturers for military vehicles also offer their products for heavy commercial vehicles, such as construction machinery or tractors, they can assume that they are exempt from export restrictions under AL 1 A. The same applies to the shipbuilding sector, where certain propulsion engines are also installed in cruise liners or container.

Needless to say, the licensing authorities will make efforts to find out what the intended use for the individual exports is, which could result in a license denial or even penalties. However, according to a study by Oxfam and the Berlin Information-centre for Transatlantic Security (BITS) large numbers of sensitive components have made their way around the world as a result of these loopholes (Nassauer & Steinmetz 2005).

58 The related export list Part 1 A includes technologies such as, military communications electronics, chemicals for weapons and fuel and numerous components for military land, sea and air vehicles.

59 Decisive in classifying a good as "specially designed for military-use" is the design intent: have there been custom-made military adaptations to the item or is it available in consumer goods catalogues. Only in the first case, the definition applies. For comparison, the US definition is more precise and states that a good that can be used unchanged for both military and dual-use purposes is categorically not a military good (Export Manager 2018, 25).

9.0 Export Control in Armament Cooperation

In the following chapter, Germany's ability to prevent the diversion of arms which are produced and traded in the context of transnational armament cooperations shall be examined. The term "ability to control" shall refer to the legal and political means to stop the trade of German goods and components outside Germany's national borders. In a second step, the study seeks to test International Relations theories by conceptualising the German stance on export controls in armament cooperations.

On 12 March 2018, the newly formed coalition Government of the SPD and CDU/CSU presented its coalition treaty. In the document the government states "we will not authorize exports to countries as long as they are directly involved in the Yemen war" (Coalition Treaty 2018, 149). Furthermore, "with a view to Yemen, we also want to reach an agreement on this restrictive export policy with our partners in the area of European joint projects". However, on 24 May 2018 the German news program Tagesschau published an article stating that German arms components will continue to be delivered to the Saudi-Coalition, as the United Kingdom struck a €6 billion deal with Qatar for the delivery of 24 Eurofighter Typhoon to which Germany will contribute essential components (Bröker & Thiels 2018). In response to a request by Left Party MP, Stefan Liebich, the Ministry of Defence explained the situation by referring to an agreement that Germany reached with the European partner nations on the Eurofighter project in December 1997. The agreement outlines the share of each country in the construction of the aircraft and other terms of conditions. The MOD did not provide the details of the document but replied "as a result, no separate approval by Germany is required for export to the Emirate of Qatar" (ibid.).

The case raises the question whether the German government could potentially intervene in the deal of another country by stopping the supply of components and whether it would want to do so.

9.1 The Eurofighter Typhoon

The Eurofighter Typhoon is Europe's largest military programme and the most expensive armament project in the history of the FRG. The first prototypes of the plane were built in 1989, yet, at the time the intention was only to build an air combat fighter. However, over the years the `Jäger 90´ evolved from the European Fighter Aircraft (EFA) and the Eurofighter 2000 to become the Multi-Role Combat Aircraft (MRCA) Eurofighter Typhoon. It is thus a multi-purpose combat aircraft that can take several roles and attack targets in the air and on the ground[60]. Serial production of the plane started in 2003 and it was commissioned in the

[60] For additional information on the history, sales and technical details of the Eurofighter, see https://www.eurofighter.com/ .

summer of 2006 (US-BW-1). The four founding nations of the project - Germany, Spain, United Kingdom and Italy - all use the aircraft in their own air forces. Furthermore, it was agreed that each of the four parent nations would host the production line and that countries would provide each other with components (just retour)[61]. This decision was a hindrance not only from an economic point of view, as having four production and assembly lines is a lot less cost-efficient than one, but it also had implications on arms export controls as the different production lines came with an intense traffic of components that have to be shipped all around Europe.

The specially created Eurofighter Jagdflugzeug GmbH is based in Halbergmoos, Bavaria. The central tasks of the company include the design, manufacture and further development of the Eurofighter Typhoon. The shareholders are BAE and EADS Deutschland with 33% each, EADS Spain (CASA) with 13% and Leonardo with 21%. The Eurofighter is manufactured in a complex interplay of seven manufacturing sites in the four cooperation countries. EADS Deutschland is building the fuselage centre section in Lemwerder, Augsburg and Manching near Ingolstadt. BAE Systems produces fuselage front parts, rear end, fins and cockpits at the Warton and Samlesbury plants and is also responsible for the software. In Cassele near Turin and Foggia, Italy, Leonardo manufactures the left wing and completes the BAE fuselage tail. In Getafe, Spain, the right wings and the slat flaps are produced. Final assembly takes place in the respective countries themselves, i.e. in Manching, Warton, Cassele and Getafe (Grässlin 2013, 228). The Eurofighter Gmbh has 400 tier one suppliers which indicates the volume of components that is transhipped across Europe for building the aircraft. In that way the Typhoon project highlights the transnational characteristics of defence trade in Europe where national borders increasingly lose their influence. It is evident that the trans-shipment of such a high volume of components poses a challenge for national export authorities given that normally, every single listed defence good must be licensed in advanced.

In order to facilitate the trade of components within international cooperation projects, the German government adjusted its regime in 1992 by introducing so-called General Licenses (GL) (§2 AWV). They are multi-year flat-rate approvals for German component deliveries to allied states. Once granted, the Federal Export Office only checks at a later stage (ex-post) how much and at what price the armaments were actually exported to the partner states. GLs for armaments of AL 1 A are granted exclusively for contracts with NATO and NATO-equivalent countries. Partners in these countries can be companies as well as multinational programme offices, as is the case of the *NATO Eurofighter and Tornado Management*

61 That principles states that countries should receive appropriate returns for the money invested in cooperative or joint programmes.

Agency (NETMA). In principle, end-use certificates are required, but are normally not requested for inter-governmental cooperations, as will be shown below.

The introduction of such licences led to a significant drop in license applications in Germany and allowed the licensing authority to focus on more sensitive cases. In practice this means that companies that supply armaments to European or NATO cooperation projects can export components without having to apply for individual licences for every good (Ger-S-2). While the introduction of GLs was intended to take care of the internal dimension by reducing the volume of licensing application, there were two further adjustments that had the goal of making Germany a more reliable partner for cooperation. This was necessary because cooperation requires a compromise between different export practices and interests of the countries participating in the joint project.

Without further regulation, if each country applied its export practice, only a minimum of exports could be authorised on the basis of the lowest common denominator, which may not be acceptable to the country with the less stringent export restrictions (Brzoska & Küchle 2002, 5)[62]. The opposite extreme would be that one country gives up their export principles and submits to the law of a cooperation country. When cooperations became more popular, the German government placed interest in cooperation projects above the interest in enforcing their own export regulations. As a result, two separate regulations were put in place that have affected the arms export control discourse until today.

9.2 Integrated Parts and Exemptions from End-Use Declarations

The first amendment to the licensing system falls under the Political Principles of 1982 where the "special interest in cooperation" is first stated. Under German law, the determination of the "end user" of components depends on whether the parts are permanently installed in a weapon system or not (AWV § 8(5)). The rule stipulated that components which are processed or integrated into a weapon system in the partner country have a new origin under German law. A fixed installation is evaluated as the "use or consumption" of a product and establishes a new origin of the product (Political Principles 1982, 4). This means that the country from which the finished weapon system is exported now has free ruling over the final destination of the German components, as such parts are usually no longer subject to German export law.

In fact, this rule can also be found in EU legislation on Dual Use trade. It reiterates the German "new-origin-after-integration rule" by stating that the "substantial and economically justifiable working or processing" of a good constitutes a

[62] In the following the author complies with the explanations of Brzoska and Küchle 2002, 7.

new origin[63]. Dual-use goods can thus be re-exported after they have been permanently installed in weapons systems abroad, without requiring the opinion of the German government. Nevertheless, there are two exceptions to this rule to safeguard German interests in exceptional cases. Firstly, if necessary, the licensing authority can set up additional regulations and oblige a company to apply for a re-export license before the goods can be reshipped (Ger-S-1). Such additional regulations are put in place for sensitive goods. Secondly, the Political Principles state that the German government may still seek to influence the export plans of their partners in a cooperative project (Political Principles 1982, Art, 3 & 5). The rule and exceptions were reproduced in the Political Principles of 2000, which means that they still form part of the German export regime today.

An additional amendment to the regime from 1996 was also concerning end-use certification. Again the idea was to assure foreign customers and cooperating partners that German parts can be purchased without having fear of re-export restrictions, while at the same time reducing licensing bureaucracy. Therefore, the Federal Security Council informed industry that there would now be a "presumption of approval" for all deliveries of weapon components for joint ventures with firms in the EU, NATO and NATO-equivalent states where German components amount to no more than 20%[64]. This relaxation also applied to other countries when the share of equipment was less than 10%. From a legal point of view, "assumption of approval" means that a company has the right to supply components and this right can only be revoked by a unanimous decision of the BMWI, the BMVg and the AA or the Federal Security Council (Federal Government 2010). The rule was based on the notion that such insignificant volumes of components would not require a re-export certification from the cooperating country and therefore increase reliability.

As a consequence, companies involved in joint projects which intended to export the final good from outside Germany could assume that German licensing authorities would only obstruct in exceptional cases. However, again, a safety clause was implemented stating that, when it comes to "significant supplies", German companies must contractually stipulate that they are to be informed of the partners' export intentions in time to give the German government the option to voice objection. The term `significant supplies´ was however broadly defined as "essential in terms of scope and significance for a weapon of war". This rule was last officially published in 2010, yet today it remains somewhat unclear how and whether it is applied.

63 In accordance with Art. 24/60 of the Customs Code of the EU (Regulation (EEC) No 2913/92; No 952/2013).

64 Exceptions include the supplies of tank engines and tank gear units, supplies to countries subject to an embargo, supplies in the field of NBC weapons or carrier technology (Federal Government 2010).

Interviews with both NGOs and industry have shown that this regulation sparks fierce debate, yet for polar-opposite reasons. On the one hand, representatives of NGOs stated that the 20% limit was no longer valid as licensing authorities today do not care how big the share of German parts are in a final product but simply authorise any supply of components to joint projects without asking for re-export certificates. As one official said, "the 20% limit is not applied anymore, nowadays German supplies to cooperation projects are warmly welcomed by the government, no questions asked" (Ger-NGO-1). On the other hand, several industry representatives voiced an opposing view, namely that the 20% rule was indeed not in place anymore but instead arguing that licensing authorities were overly restrictive so that any component would be considered significant and therefore all supplies require re-export certificates (B-I-1;2). The same was true for the majority of integrated products.

Despite these views being voiced in several interviews, their assumptions are misleading. Even though there has not been an official communication stating explicitly that this regulation was replaced, the most recent re-export control manual of BAFA (2017) does not mention the rule. This document only states that an exemption of end-use certification applies for transfers of military equipment (AL 1 A) to EU, NATO or NATO equivalent states "provided that the value of the goods does not exceed €5 000" (12). The same goes for dual-use transfers (except software) that do not exceed €10 000. In addition, exports or shipments to EU, NATO or NATO-equivalent states which have a value between €5 000 up to €125 000 merely require an Import Certificate stating officially who the importer is, which essentially means that no re-export certificate is required[65].

It appears therefore that the regulation from 1996 has been largely replaced and that it has become a political myth which is strategically employed to either voice concern or support for arms exports (cf. waffenexporte.org). In sum, while the most recent regulation limits the amount of goods that can be exported without end-use declaration to a certain financial value, the concern is still the same, namely, that certain sensitive good that are below the monetary threshold can be re-exported without the consent of the German government; this could potentially undermine the national foreign-policy. Finally, it is valuable to know whether the German government has the ability to intervene in the re-export of integrated parts that it deems "significant" and when it does so.

[65] Further exceptions are temporary exports, re-exports after importation and technology for tender purposes (BAFA 2017).

9.3 Application and Implementation of Guidelines

First of all, it appears that in terms of the "new-origin-after-integration rule", which exempts certain transfers from end-use certification, the German government has deliberately chosen not to clarify exactly what it considers a significant supply that requires further consultation. Evidence for that is that there are contradicting clauses in the Political Principles. For instance, the "new-origin-after-integration rule" (II) stands in direct opposite to the segment stating that licenses for the export of war weapons and other armaments are only granted when the end use has been assured in writing (Political Principles 2000, IV). This clause does consider any exemptions. These contradictions create ambiguity that allows for industry-friendly as well as for restrictive interpretations that politicians can use depending on their audience (US-BW-1). Furthermore, this ambiguity gives the government more freedom to act.

Interviews with export control officials have pointed to the fact that, in practice whether a component is significant depends on a variety of factors and not just on the volume or share in the final product (US-FO-2). Components that contain sensitive technology, radars, for instance are more closely monitored than others when there is risk that these goods will be shipped to a country with lax arms-control regimes. Nonetheless, the "new origin rule" means that components can be re-exported to countries to which the export of complete weapon systems would not be allowed. It appears that governments have consciously accepted risks of diversion that arise from components that can be freely traded once they have been integrated into a product. In addition, Germany relaxes end-use verification for friendly countries even though their export controls can vary significantly and sensitive goods of considerable value can be re-exported without notification to the German authorities.

Against this background, the government response to the Eurofighter inquiry is somewhat misleading as it conveys the idea that the current German government is trapped by an agreement aprevious government signed in 1996. Instead, it appears that the government consciously placed the Alliance's interest (Bündnisinteresse) above the interest to influence the destination of its military equipment. This became evident in a parliamentary inquiry by the Left Party, who asked which licences have been issued for exports to Saudi Arabia in 2015.

The response given by State Secretary Machnig yields insights into how the trade of components is handled in international cooperations:

> "Within the framework of mutual armaments cooperation, the European or American partner is dependent on the German company reliably supplying the respective components. Such export licences were granted because in the specific individual cases no foreign and security policy threat was seen as standing in the way of a legal claim by the companies. In addition, the European partner, which ultimately approves the final

> export of the finished military equipment, is also bound by the provisions of the EU Common Position" (Federal Government 2016, 3).

The statement alludes to the idea that companies have legal rights to export and that the Eurofighter deal to Qatar complies with the German and EU export principles. Yet, this is misleading for two reasons. First of all, the export broke with the obligations under the Common Position. Not only is the human rights situation in Saudi Arabia highly questionable, but additionally, because Saudi Arabia and Qatar are actively involved in the Yemen War there should have been a license denial for the export of weapons of war according to the Common Position principles.

In addition to the violation of the Common Position which has clearly taken place, the statement hides the fact that companies have no legal right to export weapons of war under German law. In fact, some of the German components that were exported in the context of the Eurofighter such as the 27mm Mausser Cannon produced by Rheinmetall, are weapons of war for which companies cannot make claims about a right to export. In addition to this, according to the Political Principles as described above the weapons of war should have been covered by end-use certificates that would have required the UK and other cooperating partners to consult the German government before re-exporting them. In that case, Germany would have had to authorise the deal too, unless the UK wanted to risk a break in foreign relations with Germany.

The analysis shows that the export of Eurofighters to Qatar is technically not aligned with the German export regime, nor with the EU Common Position. The reason for that is that such cooperation projects are regulated via specific government-to-government agreements, in a manner that avoids confrontations with national law, because the international framework agreement overrides national particularities.

9.4 International Framework Agreements

The German Federal Government has concluded framework agreements or so-called Memoranda of Understanding (MoU) with almost all NATO countries and also with non-NATO countries[66]. As the agreement of the Eurofighter is not public its content has to be derived from past MoUs. One of the first MoUs is the "Agreement on the Export of Jointly Developed and/or Manufactured War Weapons and Other Armaments" with France of 7 February 1972. It is mostly referred

[66] In response to a question which framework agreements Germany has signed, State Secretary Machnig referred to a total of 7300 agreements listed in the data base of the MoD (Federal Government 2015, 7).

to as the Schmidt Debré Convention named after the undersigning Defence Ministers.

The Schmidt Debré document is of particular interest because it is one of the few MoUs that is publicly available and it forms the basis of further agreements. The content of the 1972 agreement has become known through letters from the BMVg to defence companies and in 2000, the French version was published as an annex to a parliamentary report (Assemblé Nationale 2000). The 1972 convention provides that the governments will not prevent each other from exporting weapons of war or other armament material that was jointly produced to third countries. Furthermore, each government commits itself to granting the necessary authorisations for the supply of parts and components to the partner country. However, the Federal Government has reserved the right to refuse an authorisation if the legal situation so requires it (Section 6 KWKG). Especially under Minister of Economics, Sigmar Gabriel, several French exports have been politically blocked as they contained German components, yet it is unclear to what extent this was done on the legal basis of an MoU, or simply by exerting political pressure (Lagneau 2014).

The Schmitt/Debré convention is still valid, a fact confirmed during 2010 and 2015 parliamentary inquiries. There it was stated that the weapon systems that are mentioned under the convention namely the Transall C-160, Alpha Jet, RATAC, Hot, Milan and Roland weapons systems, as well as future developments of these weapons, will be covered by the agreement unless other special agreements are made (Federal Government 2015)[67]. Other inter-governmental agreements were made in the same spirit, most notably the Farnborough Agreement from July 2000[68]. It was signed by all European countries with major defence capabilities and sets out how the European defence base can be restructured in the future in order to remain competitive. Under Part 3 which deals with Transfer and Export Procedures, the document stipulates that all parties shall establish, at the beginning of a project, what kinds of weapon systems can be exported to which countries. Later revisions can only be made by a unanimous decision. Furthermore, "a permitted Export destination may only be removed in the event of significant changes in its internal situation, for example full scale civil war or a serious deterioration of the human rights situation" (Farnborough 2000, Article 13[3]). While the document provides for a consultation procedure, it does not contain the right

67 Today, the Schmidt/Debré MoU only applies to the successor of the Milan tank-guided missile as the other goods are not produced anymore (Federal Government 2015). Furthermore, negotiations for a successor MoU are currently part of the public discourse (cf. Treaty of Achen 2019).

68 Original title: Framework Agreement between the French Republic, the Federal Republic of Germany, the Italian Republic, the Kingdom of Spain, the Kingdom of Sweden, and the United Kingdom concerning Measures to facilitate the Restructuring and Operation of the European Defence Industry.

to veto an export. Moreover, it contains a significant relaxation of export controls by stating that the use of government issued end-use certificates shall be minimised in favour of company certificates of use[69].

The Typhoon programme is also covered by an MoU and several interviews have shown that it is based on the same principles as the Farnborough and Schmidt/Debré agreements, with only slight variations (US-BW-1;2). Most importantly, the MoU contains clauses that prevent states from interfering with each other's export politics and also an obligation for a country that wants to intervene in a deal by a partner country to cover the resulting costs. In order to understand why Germany would be willing to let others freely export German technology in such projects, it is necessary to understand the political and economic context of such large-scale armament collaborations. As a member of the German Foreign Office said, "I don't remember ever having rejected a request for the export of the Typhoon in four years" (US-FO-1).

There are two related explanations for this: despite its strong military capability, the export of Eurofighters poses relatively small foreign policy and security risks for states. This is due to the fact that the majority of so-called pariah states can neither afford nor operate or maintain such a high-tech plane. In fact, weapon systems like the Eurofighter "cannot just be put on someone's door step like any other parcel delivery" (US-BW-2). Moreover, such deals include special training contracts involving the military of the selling country who must go and train the forces of the buyer country on the weapons. It is important to note that large scale contracts such as for aircrafts or submarines are quite different from smaller contracts or the trade of components for mostly economic reasons.

For deals like the Eurofighter, industry and government often align to promote their product in order to beat the international competition. Especially in the aircraft domain there is a strong level of competition with France's Rafale, Sweden's Gripen and the US F-35 stealth fighter. Furthermore, it takes years and huge amounts of money to develop such a defence project. Since the four Eurofighter countries are unable to exploit economies of scale and learning just from their national demand they rely on exports in order to make the project economically viable. This creates pressure for governments to export. Before the deals with Saudi Arabia and Qatar came through, BAE systems announced to set off 2000 employees due to low demand in Eurofighters (Kollewe 2017). Yet, not only are job losses at stake but also a potential loss of expertise, because it is increasingly difficult to maintain high-skilled personnel if demand for airplanes drops. This explains why states have no interest in preventing one another from exporting and why Germany has relaxed its export principles for cooperation programmes.

69 Upon ratification, Germany added it would not accept this provision and continue to use government EUCs.

9.5 Evaluation: Armament Cooperation

The study on armament cooperation and component trade has yielded insights into several risks of diversion. Firstly, the "new-origin-after-integration rule" can lead to situations in which a transferred good gets transhipped further without the German government's approval. Secondly, the exemption from declaring end-use for goods that are under a certain monetary value can have the consequence that goods, which may not be high in value but which can still be very sensitive, are transhipped via allied partners without opportunities for the government to intervene. Finally, the experience with government MoUs has shown that Germany trades its stricter export criteria for economic reasons and alliance interests. This situation is problematic as neither the restrictive Policy Principles from 2000 nor the embargo to the Saudi-Led coalition can be implemented consistently within the framework of international arms cooperation.

One instrument to reduce the risk of diversion resulting from re-exports could be to make German supplies from NATO, EU and NATO-equivalent countries generally subject to authorisation, even if a new origin of goods is created by permanent installation. In this area, there is a significant difference to US arms export law, where a re-export licence must always be applied for defence articles (22 US Code 2778, Section 123.10). Under the US International Traffic in Arms Regulations (ITAR), individual licenses are required for all defence exports and transfers. In addition, ITAR imposes extraterritorial control on exports of weapons systems containing components which are covered by ITAR, irrespective of those component's share of the value of the system (ibid). Furthermore, in the past the US principles have rarely been compromised even in cooperation projects[70]. The example shows that such regulation is possible and moreover that Germany could do more to endorse a restrictive arms export policy[71].

Finally, this case study gives reason to think that the diversion of arms in the context of armament cooperation is a result of rational government choices and only indirectly attributable to globalisation. As such, the factors that have forced European governments into cooperating such as inflation of military equipment, the drop in demand, and pressure to export are linked to globalisation, however, the German government's choice to renounce its export control criteria for the sake of cooperation is not directly linked to the transnationalisation of industry or forms of hyper-globalisation.

---

70 An exception is provided by the UK-US Defence Trade Cooperation Deal that entered into force in 2012. It appears that here the US has relaxed its stricter regulations to some extent to favour cooperation with the UK.

71 It is difficult to predict to what degree German participation in cooperation would decline as a result of introducing more restrictive measurements.

9.6 Theorising Armament Cooperation

From a theoretical perspective, the German approach to governing arms exports in cooperation contains elements of liberalism, neo-realism and the political ideology of economic liberalism. Liberal thinking is reflected in the idea that the state gives up a large degree of strategic autonomy over arms production because it will generate more relative gains for itself and its allies. In addition, being a reliable cooperating partner is generally valued above the importance of enforcing one's own foreign policy or ethical principles as well as design interests, because cooperation with others will lead to mutual security benefits. These mutual security benefits are for instance, interoperability of military equipment, which generally strengthens the allies´ ties and the peace-seeking institutions to which they are members, such as NATO or the EU.

In addition, there are also absolute gains from such cooperation and respectively an underlying neo-liberal or economic liberal rationale[72]. This is based on the idea that cooperation with other states will increase return on investment and help exploit economies of scale and learning. Cooperation with other countries and their militaries automatically generates more demand for the Eurofighter and more combined power to win (and influence) export contracts. This in turn increases the numbers of planes produced and therefore reduces the unit price of each plane. The consequence is a significant reduction of costs which could not be achieved if one country produced the plane by itself. Moreover, it is unlikely that Germany would have the industrial capacity to produce such a plane alone and therefore it is bound to either cooperate with, or buy from European partners or the US. Given that buying from others would weaken Germany's military-industrial base and that Germany would only be a junior partner in cooperation with the US, as a result of American dominance in the military industrial sector, it appears to be a rational decision to cooperate with European allies.

However, there is a limit to the explanatory power of this prism. Firstly, neoliberalist market thinking would assume that states divide production assets in an efficient and cooperative way since this would create the largest economic gains for everyone. This is however not done in the Eurofighter project, where final assembly takes place in each partner country and not where it is most efficient. The second element that contradicts this view is that countries assert their prerogatives when it comes to the export of the final product. The logic of self-help - meaning that states seek their own interests and will not subordinate them to that of other states - takes precedence over alliance interests. The balance between economic and alliance interests on the one hand, and security interests on the other, shifts in favour of the latter as the security and economic relevance of a certain good or component rises.

---

72 Traditional liberalism is concerned with relative gains whereas neo-liberalists believe that states are, or should be, concerned with absolute gains (Moravcsik 1997).

In a neo-realist wording, one could say cooperation among states is limited by fears of relative gains made by other states that could threaten one's security and independence. Applied to export control this means that the countries participating in the Eurofighter consortium fear that a shared management of final export decisions may undermine their national foreign-policy and security interests. As all European states participating in the joint project are more or less equally situated within the international structure, no state can impose its interests on others. As a result, clear rules need to be established – in the form of MoUs – that ensure that states have sovereign power over final exports so that no conflicts arise. Only a combination of liberal and realist thinking can explain export control in international armament cooperation.

Finally, it can be predicted that cooperation will increase as the inflation of military equipment increases to an extent that governments abandon the `juste retour´ principle and give up their sovereignty over final exports simply for economic reasons.

10.0 Sub-licensing

In April 2015, pictures from a fiercely embattled Yemen spread, showing Saudi military aircrafts dropping boxes of equipment over Aden airport. The gear was given to groups fighting the Houthi rebels, and it quickly became clear that the delivery involved G3 assault rifles from the German manufacturer Heckler & Koch (HK). Furthermore, in January 2016 Al-Qaeda published a video that showed their combatants in various towns in Yemen firing German G36, MG3 and MG4 rifles. These four small arms appear in dozens of videos and they were almost exclusively exported to or produced under license in Saudi Arabia. In fact, the Saudi government has been allowed to produce the G3 under licence since 1969 and its newer version, the G36 since 2008, yet only for the needs of its own military (Gebauer 2015a). Moreover, HK has exported MG3 and MG4 weapons to the Royal family over years, but without permission to re-export. The presence of these arms in Yemen has led to consternation among the political class: not only does it further escalate the humanitarian crisis, but it also raises questions to what extent the small-arms exports and license production pose a foreign and security policy risk.

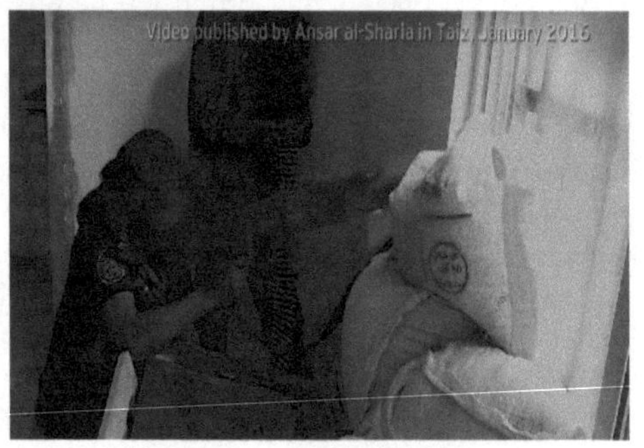

Figure 9: Diverted MG3 in Yemen
Source: Deutsche Welle (2018)

For this reason, the Green Party asked for further information from the government on the case. In response, the economics department admitted that "a physical end-use control of the G3 and G36 manufactured in Saudi Arabia" was "not possible on the basis of the underlying permits" (ibid.). The government's response is brief, but meaningful. It states that when the German arms factory was delivered to Saudi Arabia in 2008, a declaration was obtained from the royal family that it would only use the licensed weapons for the personal use of the Saudi Arabian security forces. However, it was agreed that an "on-site inspection" would require the consent of the Kingdom. The Saudi government showed little will to cooperate when the German government confronted it with the case in 2015.

Due to the absence of any will to investigate these diversions on the Saudi side, the German government seems to only have limited means to find out how the small arms had been diverted and how to prevent this in the future. The diversion of HK weapons to Yemen raises a number of questions: how effective are end-use declarations and controls? And are there legal or political ways to halt license production when the license-taker violates the contract?

In order to answer these questions, it is necessary to take a look at the structure of the small-arm sector and to identify the policy stance the German government has towards license production of small arms.

10.1 Small Arms: Market and Perceptions

The structure of the global small-arm market is different from that of complex weapon systems, such as combat planes. This is because small arms are much easier to operate, a lot to cheaper to produce and the barrier to enter the market is lower. The production of the Eurofighter, for instance, is hardly comparable to that of a sub-machine gun in terms of the level of technology and expertise that is required. However, this does not mean that anyone can easily produce very sophisticated small arms. In fact, the quality of products varies strongly and there are a lot fewer companies which can produce very sophisticated small arms fit for military use that withstand all sorts of weather conditions (GER-NGO-1).

According to the most recent report by UN funded Small-Arms-Survey, there are currently more than 1 billion firearms spread around the world, with an annual production of around 700 000 [73] (Karp 2017, 5). These are produced by more than 1 000 companies from some 100 countries (ibid). Consequently, there exists a

---

[73] The focus of this case study is only on small arms and not on light weapons. According to the OSCE Document on Small Arms and Light Weapons (2012), small arms are broadly categorized as those weapons intended for use by individual members of armed or security forces. They include revolvers, rifles, sub-machine guns etc. Light weapons are broadly categorized as those weapons intended for use by several members of armed or security forces serving as a crew. They include heavy machine guns; mounted grenade launchers; portable anti-aircraft guns and anti-tank guns and mortars of calibres less than 100 mm etc. (2).

diverse array of products in this sector and a large variety of sellers, unlike in other defence sectors where there are only a handful producers, especially in Europe. In 2014, the top five exporters of small arms were: the United States, Italy, Brazil, Germany and South Korea[74]. The top importers were the United States, Canada, Indonesia, Saudi Arabia and Germany (ibid)[75]. This shows that Germany is the dominant European player in that industrial sector, however, it is important to note that the trade of small arms in Germany constituted less than 1% of all arms exports in monetary terms in 2016[76]. Hence, this sector carries only an extremely small economic weight.

A special structural feature of the sector is related to the fact that, depending on national arms-control practices, in some countries there is also a civilian market for such weapons. While Germany strictly limits small-arms possession to sporting arms and hunting weaponry, laws in other countries, such as the US, pose very few restrictions. A survey of 56 countries found that 857 million small arm weapons (85% of global small arms) are held by civilians, 40% of which by American citizens (Holtom & Pavesi 2017). In contrast, comparatively few arms are in military arsenals (133 million – 13%), or are owned by law enforcement agencies (23 million – 2%). Aside from the industrial market there is a large black market for small arms. According to the UN around 25% of small-arms trade is illicit or not recorded as by law.

In recent years there has been strong political opposition to small arms sales due to the security risks associated. An estimated 50 000 to 100 000 people are killed every year by SALW. This can predominantly be attributed to their wide circulation both in areas of conflict and elsewhere (BpB 2012). In addition, a Red Cross study of 41 conflict areas found that out of 100 casualties on average: two are killed by hand grenades, five by large weapon system, ten by landmines, ten by artillery and mortars, ten by pistols and the remaining 63 by rifles (Herby 1999; Grässlin 2013, 412).

In this respect, former UN Secretary General Kofi Annan stated in 2006 that "in terms of the carnage they cause, small arms, indeed, could well be described as `weapons of mass destruction´" (BpB 2012.). This is why the restriction of small-arms sales and more transparency has been in the focus of NGO engagements and strongly contributed to the introduction of the Arms Trade Treaty (2014). The German government has welcomed the implementation of restrictive

74 Countries are listed in descending order.

75 The report is based on UN Comtrade data which captures international commercial activity, however, it relies on state's transparency which was especially low for countries such as China and Saudi Arabia and which are believed to be among the top exporters too.

76 While total exports of Germany were worth €6.8 billion in 2016, only €47.8 million accounted for small arms. Globally, the small arm trade was $6 billion in 2014 (ammunition accounted for 38% of global transfers).

measures and amended its export control regime in response to the ATT. In addition, according to UN studies it is the most transparent country when it comes to small-arms sales (Holtom & Pavesi 2017, 44).

10.2 Government Stance and Policy

HK is the largest small-arm producer in Germany and according to its own sources, the leading international firm when it comes to the production of rifles, grenade launchers and military pistols (HK Report 2018, 6). The company is most known for providing the German military with G36 rifles and P8 pistols, however, it also provides firearms to several police and military units such as the British SAS, the US Navy SEALs and the German GSG9 and KSK[77]. As a result of the positive economic outlook, the company has initiated a "strategic reorientation" towards more ethical exports to so-called "green countries". This is an in-house classification of countries that takes into account human rights criteria (HK Report 2018)[78].

However, the statement also indicates that HK used to pursue a different strategy that did not make ethical distinctions between states. In the past, the company struggled financially and there were several instances in which HK was close to bankruptcy. HK has been involved in an extensive list of lawsuits, related to accusations of corruption and illicit trade[79]. The lowest point of the company's relations with the government was in 2015 when German Minister of Defence, Ursula Von der Leyen decided to withdraw 167 000 G36 rifles from service due to insufficient accuracy when exposed to high heat. In the context of the discord between the company and its most important customer - the German government - the change in strategy can also be seen as a way to improve relations and polish up the company's image by employing non-market strategies. In general, the government support for the small arms industry has dropped.

While in the years after WWII and during the cold war the German government had an interest in supporting its small-arm industry for economic and foreign-policy reasons, this support has become weaker as Germany gradually reduced its defence spending and strengthened its role as normative actor. In 2015, in response to the Arms Trade Treaty (ATT), the German government further re-

---

77 In September 2016 the French DGA awarded HK a contract to supply the French Army with the HK 416F as replacement of the FAMAS. The contract was signed for 15 years and covers 102.000 units with a value of €140 million (HK Report 2018, 13).

78 (i) the Corruption Perception Index by Transparency International, (ii) the Democracy Index by Economist Intelligence Unit and (iii) whether the buying country is a NATO or a NATO-equivalent state.

79 Most recently HK members were on trial for having illicitly trafficked arms to provinces inside Mexico which were excluded from the export license of G36.

stricted small and light weapons (SALW) exports to third states with the introduction of the so-called *Small Arm Principles*. The major changes included that no export licenses would be granted for new production lines of SALW in Third States so that the recipient's capacities would not be expanded (Small Arm Principles 2015, 2).

Therefore, a "new for old principle" was introduced which requires that for every new shipment of SALW, the former weapons must be destroyed (ibid.). In addition, the government did not list small arms as a key technology in their *Strategy Paper for the Strengthening of the German Defence Industry* (2015). This means that Germany is not willing to maintain small arm technology, but instead is prepared to buy it on the European or global market. Consequently, HK cannot rely on government support anymore in the form of targeted research and technology programmes, or in terms of procurement and export support. The introduced restrictions directly affect HK's ability to make profit in the future.

In fact, Germany has not always had such a restrictive stance, as is illustrated by the evolution of license production. To begin with, the most widespread small arm in the world is the AK-47 Kalashnikov, directly followed by HK's Gewehr 3. The G3 was developed in the context of a joint project between the German and the Spanish government in the 1950s, for which the German government contracted HK and Mauser and the Spanish government the company CETME[80]. Germany then purchased the sales rights in 1959 and assigned production to HK[81]. The consequence of the government deal with Spain was that the German State was the license holder and not an individual company (B-I-3). The Federal Government chose to award contracts to friendly states - the first one being Portugal in 1961. While HK was able to make large profits through exports of the weapon or providing technical assistance for establishing production lines, the revenues for the license went directly into the pockets of the government (Grässlin 2013). However, this strategy caused immense backlash when Portuguese Dictator, Antonio de Oliveira Salazar, used the G3 to beat down protests in African colonies and it became public that the German government financially benefitted. In addition, the Portuguese produced many more units than allowed and exported them wherever they wished.

In total, it is estimated that the G3 was produced under license in 15 countries, of which only a few (Iran & Turkey) still produce it today (Widman 2014). Nowadays, military forces have largely replaced the G3 with the updated version, namely, HK's G36. Since 1958, HK weapons have been exported legally to at least 88 countries (ibid.). Yet, the experiences of license production from 1960 to 1980 have had repercussions on Germany's small-arms policy today.

---

80 Centro de Estudios Técnicos de Materiales Especiales

81 At first production was assigned to both Rheinmetall and HK, yet in the late 1970s, production rights were given only to HK (B-I-2).

There are two changes in the German government's policy agenda that can be attributed to these experiences. Firstly, the government has refrained from owning Intellectual Property (IP) and sales rights of weapon technology and, secondly, it stopped conducting government-to-government deals[82]. In addition, the stance towards license production in autocratic regimes has changed. The following analysis of the policy agenda on small arms, coupled with complimentary interviews on their implementation, shall serve to answer the overarching question: whether diversions as a result of license production abroad can be prevented under the current framework.

10.3 Restriction on the Delivery of Key Components

A first protective measure that was implemented into licensing agreements, such as the one with the Saudi Government, is a clause stating that certain key components which are necessary for final assembly must be delivered from Germany. In that way, the government reserves for itself the ability to stop the production of weapons in case the license-taking country does not comply with the end-use declaration. In case of the Saudi deal, for instance, the gun barrel and the lock had to be delivered by HK from Germany (Ger-NGO-1). After the diversions were revealed and the embargo put in place, the government made use of this clause and halted the delivery of these components (ibid.). Needless to say, this caused loud protests on the Saudi side, yet, this does not necessarily mean that the measure has been effective in stopping the G36 production. This is because there are several strategies that states and industry can undertake in order to mitigate security of supply issues in an effort to decrease dependency on the supplier.

Firstly, they can seek autarky by investing in R&D in order to independently develop the component (James 2019). The example of the Mexican assault rifle FX-05, almost an exact copy of the German G36 illustrates how this is possible. Mexico had originally produced the G3 in license and agreed to replace that production with its successor the G36. However, before the deal was concluded, Mexico managed to copy the HK technology and manufacture a weapon that is almost identical in terms of shot cadence, calibre and appearance. This led to a law suit for technology theft from which HK however stepped back, perhaps in exchange for the G36 deal mentioned above. In this technological era, when weapons and their components can be printed via 3D printers, there is an increased risk that partial technology transfer, as it happens in the context of sub-licensing, can lead to intellectual property and technology theft. The Mexican example also poses a risk for the Saudi case as it allows the Saudi government to diversify the

[82] Even during the Eurofighter Deal with Austria, the German Air force sold the planes it had purchased back to EADS, so that it would not be a direct sale from the German to the Austrian government (US-BW-2).

supply chain i.e. to get similar components from other countries producing such weapons.

Another strategy that countries pursue is stockpiling the component or material. During interviews with NGOs it was said that the Saudi production line faced several problems at first so that the Saudi government ordered direct exports of G36 weapons from Germany to fulfil its demand (Ger-NGO-1). The locks and barrels that were not assembled were allegedly stockpiled, which may have allowed the continuation of production after the embargo. In fact, the German government had to admit that it did not know how many of the 20 000 G36 sets (and tens of millions worth of spare parts) had been assembled over time (Gebauer 2015a). Yet, whether stockpiling was a deliberate strategy pursued in anticipation of security of supply risks arising from the Yemen involvement cannot be finally validated.

Furthermore, there has not been sufficient evidence on whether the Saudi Government has pursued other ways to bypass the sources of constraint, nonetheless, the example shows that halting the delivery of key components is not to be seen as an effective catch-all provision and cannot necessarily prevent countries from producing a certain weapon. Once the production line and parts of the technological know-how have been provided, it becomes increasingly difficult to prevent countries from producing small arms by means of stopping component supply.

10.4 Legal Impediments

A second aspect that could undermine the German government's ability to stop license production is related to the German legal system. In order to prevent a law-suit the German government did not deny license decisions for the export of components in 2014 but merely put them on hold in order to buy time. Nonetheless, HK took the German government to court for "failure to act" in an effort to force the government into taking a decision (Zeit 2016). On 23 June 2016 the Administrative Court in Frankfurt ruled that the company had a right to a timely decision and that further hesitation by the government was not permissible (Gebauer 2016). In response to the ruling the company amended its charge with the aim to oblige the German government to permit the exports that were put on hold (ibid.). It would thus be a legal question and up to the courts to decide if component delivery can continue or not.

The ruling of the court will in part depend on whether the key components are classified as "weapons of war" under the KWKG or as "other armaments" under the AWG. In the latter case, the government would have the duty to prove that the export of these goods threatens national security, the peaceful coexistence of people, or disrupts German foreign relations (cf. 8.0 Legal Ambiguities). As interviews have shown, this is not an easy task, especially since the German government itself said that there is not enough evidence that the arms were deliberately diverted by the Saudi Government (US-FO-1).

It is worth noting that such a situation is more likely to happen in Germany than in countries where governments still have a significant share in the company and can therefore influence business decisions directly. Based on the German legal system the government cannot freely decide on restricting the export of goods that are crucial for the assembly of a weapon of war, such as parts of a machine gun. The burden of proof lies with the government Specifically, when it comes to goods that cannot clearly be assigned to the KWKG. This gives companies a significant amount of bargaining power to legally enforce exports.

10.5 Post-Shipment Controls

Finally, the G36 diversion via Saudi Arabia led to a reform of the arms exports control regime, initiated mainly by Minister for Economic Affairs, Sigmar Gabriel in 2015. Instead of relying on written end-user declaration by governments, which had been common practice, Minister Gabriel was eager to introduce "on-site end-use verification controls". This means that members of the Foreign Office and BAFA would check whether the exported goods were used only for the agreed purpose, in the agreed region. In an interview an SPD spokesman said that in the past governments had been "somewhat naïve" when it came to approving license productions. Post-shipment controls were formally introduced by a BAFA announcement from 1 August 2017 and over the course of two years there have been controls in India, the United Arab Emirates and in South Korea. However, only in the case of India did the government reveal what the subject of control was, namely sniper rifles; furthermore, it was said that "they were all at the designated location" (BR 2017).

Today, pistols and rifles can only be sold abroad if the recipients confirm that the goods remain in their own country. Moreover, an agreement that controls may take place on site must be obtained by recipients in third countries. The introduction of post-shipment controls has been suggested by NGOs for years but was rejected by all previous governments, who argued that Germany's end-use declarations were among the strictest in the world and therefore sufficient (Federal Government 2010, 2). The introduction of additional controls now puts these statements into question. Nevertheless, in international comparison Germany demonstrates a high level of transparency and a strict application of end-use declaration (cf. Bromley & Griffiths 2010). The BAFA guide on how these documents are to be handled stretches over 24 pages and it is of international repute. Moreover, with the USA and Switzerland, Germany is one of the few countries in the world that conducts on-site controls, which is an indicator for the restrictiveness of the German control regime (Knöpfle 2017). The question remains whether this approach can be effective in practice?

On this point, all interviewees have voiced doubts that the post shipment controls will put an end to diversion of German small arms. One reason that was voiced repeatedly is related to the fact that controls are not conducted in NATO states, such as the US, which in the past often transferred German arms to unstable states or even paramilitary groups that were not able to safeguard them in the long-term (US-BW-1;2)[83]. A second issue in the implementation is related to limited capacity and expertise when it comes to conducting the controls. A small inquiry by the Left Party revealed that only two posts have been created at the responsible BAFA in order to carry out controls (Prössl 2018). This seems hardly sufficient to control the whereabouts of small arms in countries around the world. However, in the past, BAFA coordinated with German embassies in conducting controls before a good got shipped (ex-ante), which is actually often omitted from academic and public discussion.

Interviews with members of the economics department of the German Embassy in Washington have revealed insights into the implementation of such controls. Interviewees said that, "very occasionally" the embassy is tasked to visit production sites to gather information on how the exported good would be used. In most instances, one person would then be sent to the importing company in order to conduct an onsite inspection (US-FO-3). There are several issues that arise though.

Firstly, members of the Foreign Office are generalists and not arms-control experts. Therefore, it is very possible that a person without prior knowledge of arms control is tasked with post-shipment control. One interviewee said about his visit to a factory "they could have told me anything, I had no clue about the product and the risks associated with it" (US-FO-3). Furthermore, members of the Foreign Office rotate every three years, which makes it hard for them to familiarise themselves with the local economic environment and anticipate particular risks of diversion. Due to the fact that there have been neither increases in personnel nor systemic changes that would allow for expert controls, the political will behind this new tool is questionable. This notion is enforced by the fact that in two years there have only been visits to three countries, excluding countries that are said to have a strong record in diverting arms, such as Saudi Arabia. In contrast, under the US Blue-Lantern Programme, 570 checks for 1.3% of licence applications have been conducted in 2015 (State Department 2016, 4). Furthermore, since 1990 over 14 400 checks have been conducted in 80 - 100 countries per year (ibid.).

83 The German government also gave around 30 000 small arms to Peschmerga rebels to support them in their fight against ISIS in 2014. Given that these weapons can be operated for more than 40 years there is a high risk of diversion from that too (Herby 1999).

In the context of the quantitative and qualitative indicators, it is not surprising that interviewees voiced little faith in the effectiveness of the German controls. This is also because countries must consent to the controls and must agree to have inspectors on the premises of their companies or military bases. This is a question of soft power where the strongest often wins, as in the case of the US. On the one hand, the US has extremely strict post-shipment controls[84], however, interviewees stated that it would be unimaginable that the US government would consent to having a foreign delegation inspect the equipment on their own military bases (US-BW-2). The imbalance of power is further illustrated by the fact that in Germany, US government officials would at times arrive at military bases and insist on conducting post-shipment controls without having informed the authorities beforehand[85].

What is worth dwelling on is that there is no international law that obligates Germany to admit to these controls, yet, the fear of US sanctions is apparently enough to pressure countries into consenting. If one applies this rationale to German controls, it becomes clear that Germany will only be able to conduct controls in countries where it has sufficient soft power to compel them to accept such controls. Against this backdrop it appears difficult to further expand the controls from small arms to larger war weapons and their components, as unlike with small arms such component controls would require inspections into the technological heart of a given machine. It is likely that not only the US but that other countries too would reject such controls on national security grounds.

The effectiveness of post-shipment controls was summed up as follows: "it may create more hurdles for those that agree to it, but those who want to divert weapons will not be held back by this measure" (US-FO-3).

10.6 Evaluation: License Production of Small Arms

The case study has shown that end-use declarations have no effect when the signing government has an interest in diverting arms. In addition, sub-license production poses the risk of unwanted technology transfer which creates economic as well as security risks. This is, however, only in part attributable to globalisation. For instance, due to the contracted small-arms market and the large number of sellers in this field, buyer countries such as Saudi Arabia are able to attach more conditions to contracts. Often this involves a partial transfer of technology rights and the request to have parts of the value chain take place on national grounds – so-called offsets. This creates a heightened risk of diversion. Keeping control over

84 During interviews the example was given that if a decommissioned German helicopter uses an American radar and is given to a German museum, it is possible that the radar must be removed because this new purpose of the helicopter was not in the initial agreement (US-BW-1).

85 "The US is not eager to make compromises in this domain; we still try to get them to inform us before knocking on our doors and asking where their things are" (US-BW-2).

the delivery of key components has the potential to limit these risks. Yet, due to the particularities of the German law, this security-policy decision can be undermined by an administrative court.

Another decisive factor will depend on the German government's willingness to allocate resources to enforcing post-shipment controls. Under the current framework it is rather unlikely to have a significant impact as more qualified personnel would be required. Furthermore, it remains to be seen whether German Governments will insist on such controls and thus employ soft power to make international partners consent to their conditions. Finally, the Federal government treats the trade of small arms rather differently from cooperation projects. The *Small Arms Principles* as well as *the Strategy Paper for the Strengthening of the German Defence Industry* from 2015 highlight a rather restrictive policy stance where the government is less willing to give up sovereign control.

10.7 Theorising License Production of Small Arms

It appears that small-arms licensing can be explained most appropriately by an interplay of neo-realist and constructivist notions. Granting a license to another country is not based on the same cooperative rationale as jointly producing armament goods such as the joint Eurofighter project. This is because license production such as the G36 in Saudi Arabia, is not predominantly aimed at strengthening a political alliance, nor is the goal to achieve interoperability. Instead, the logic of self-help prevails, which means that license production is mostly granted in order to maximise one's own security by helping others – such as Saudi Arabia - to balance out a common threat, which for several years was the Soviet Union and Iran.

Furthermore, the notion of mutual benefits is also different. The deal with Saudi Arabia is not focussed on the exploitation of economies of scale and learning, nor is it grounded in the idea that the maintenance of small-arms industry is crucial for national security concerns. Instead, it is a result of an inevitable dependency where Germany has an interest in maintaining good relations in order to keep Saudi Arabia as a major customer of its goods and services and to ensure access to its oil resources. Measures to intervene in the production process are also based on a neo-realist rationale as the use of German small arms against allies of Germany can potentially undermine Germany's role in the international system, which may outweigh the interest in maintaining good ties with Saudi Arabia.

However, the power-maximising rationale is also limited in its explanatory power, especially when it comes to aspects such as the arms embargo and the introduction of the Small Arm Principles and Post-Shipment Controls. A neo-realist reading would have assumed that Germany continues to sell arms to Saudi Arabia as neither the murder of Khashoggi nor the attacks in Yemen pose a direct threat to German security that would justify a stop in trade relations and a reduction in German influence. In fact, in the past, human rights violations have not led to a change in German foreign policy precisely because it would have run counter the neo-realist interest in preserving power. For instance, neither the reoccurring information on torture and arbitrary executions, nor the Saudi's military suppression of protests in Bahrain in 2011 have affected German foreign policy towards the country. However, with the embargo in 2018, Germany broke with that thinking and `freely´ decided to renounce gains from maintaining good trade relations with Saudi Arabia – at least temporarily. These decisions are better explained by employing a constructivist lens. Constructivism suggests that states are neither unitary actor nor are they driven by rational or natural interests. Instead, the identities, values and norms of a society's core actors form the basis of state interest. Based on such a reading, the introduction of the Small Arm Principles, as a result of the Arms Trade Treaty negotiations, was "determined primarily by shared ideas rather than material forces" (Wendt 1999, 1).

In addition, the introduction of an arms embargo on Saudi Arabia is an expression of the values and norms of core actors in German society which have pushed back material interests. Yet given the general dependency on the Saudi Oil and purchasing power it is likely that neo-realist thinking will prevail in the long-term.

11.0 Affiliated Companies and Joint Ventures

The final case study shall focus on Germany's biggest defence company, Rheinmetall, and two of its affiliates in Italy and South Africa with the goal to analyse to what extent their trade activities could undermine German export policy. Furthermore, the aim is to find out what the German government stance is on controlling national companies abroad. Despite the government's decision to stop arms exports to Saudi Arabia, Rheinmetall continues to deliver weapons and ammunition, which was revealed by several newspapers in December 2018 (Handelsblatt 2018; Zeit 2018). The trade relations between the Royal family, and the Italian Rheinmetall subsidiary RWM Italia already caused a stir in 2017 when the New York Times released a video called "How did bombs made in Italy kill a family in Yemen?" (Browne et al. 2017). The video showed that the major bombs used in Yemen – American MK 80 General Purpose Bombs – are produced by Rheinmetall subsidiaries. Specifically, the affiliate RWM Italia located in Sardinia and the joint venture with Denel Ammunitions (RDM) based in South Africa have since been the focus of interest as they are Rheinmetall's major ammunition plants abroad.

The revelations triggered a scandal in Italy and Germany and it raised the question of who is responsible for the sale of American bombs that are produced in Italy and sold to Saudi Arabia by German-owned companies. In a TV interview,

Italian Minister of Defence, Roberta Pinotti denied responsibility, as did the German government through several statements (Grüll & Hoffman 2018). However, from a legal point of view the question is clear: the country of production is responsible for authorising the exports and only has to consult foreign governments if the export involves foreign technology. Since the MK 80 series is a sub-license contract from the US firm Raytheon, the German government had no say in this decision (Nassauer 2018). Moreover, contrary to Ms Pinotti's television statement, there has been proof that the sales were in fact authorised by the Italian government and therefore not sent illegally. In order to fully understand the challenges that affiliate companies can bring to national governments, an analysis of Rheinmentall's trade activities abroad will be conducted.

Figure 10: Sana'a school bus attack involving US MK 82

Source: Mint Press News (2018)
©Ole Solvang/ Human Rights Watch

Figure 11: MK 83-bomb by RWM Italia found in Saada

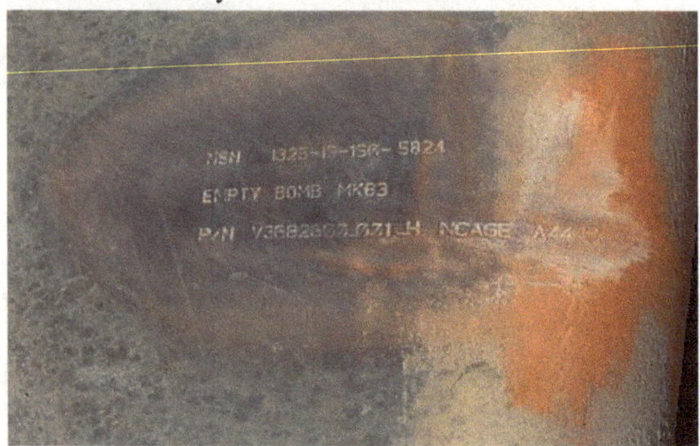

Source: Nassauer (2018)
© Ahmed Abdulkareem/MPN News

11.1 The Structure of the Rheinmetall Group

Rheinmetall ranks 26th on the global scale of defence companies and it is the largest defence contractor in Germany. However, the firm makes the vast majority of its revenues outside of Germany (72.3% in 2018) and employs 50.3% of its employees abroad. Such a strong dependency on sales abroad is not usually the case for big defence players, which are sometimes almost completely funded by the national government of their country of origin (cf. Northrop Grumman). Rheinmetall's defence sector accounts for about 60% of sales, which in 2018 amounted to €3 221 million (Annual Report 2019)[86]. Within the defence sector, the weapons and ammunition segment accounts for about 32% of all defence revenues[87].

According to the companies own evaluation, it ranks among the top five in the world in its product range and possesses technological leadership in the weapon and ammunition segment (Schwer 2013, 28). Given that Rheinmetall's L/44 and L/55 tank guns are standard worldwide and that much of its ammunition is produced by other manufacturers around the world this seems plausible. For instance, the Rheinmetall tank guns are not only used in Leopard tanks, but also in the newer American Abrams tanks, in the Japanese T90, in the current South Korean tanks and in Israeli Merkavas.

Over the years the company has pursued an offensive internationalisation strategy. In 2018 the company report states 120 locations worldwide of which 41 are in Germany. Furthermore, the company concluded sales in 144 countries and shows a strong level of market integration. One indicator for this is that Rheinmetall AG has direct or indirect holdings in 189 companies abroad and in Germany and a total of 151 companies are fully consolidated in the consolidated financial statements, among which are also RWM Italia and Denel Ammunitions (Annual Report 2019, 20).

The high level of foreign ownership and the strong dependency on foreign sales highlights the transnational structure of the company for which the German government only accounts for a quarter of sales. The subsidiaries abroad are crucial to the company's sales strategy as they give access to foreign markets. This is also validated by the strong revenues that the foreign affiliate and joint venture have recently achieved. Revenue at RWM Italia grew 50% in 2016, and out of 489 million total exports, 440 million are related to bomb sales from the MK 80 series

86 The company is divided into two corporative sectors: defence and automotive.

87 The other two segments that constitute the company's defence sector, namely vehicle systems and electronic solutions, accounted for 41% and 19% in 2018.

to Saudi Arabia[88]. Furthermore, the joint venture with RDM has achieved a six-fold increase in sales since 2008, more than 80% of which go abroad[89].

Figure 12: MK 80 series General Purpose Bomb

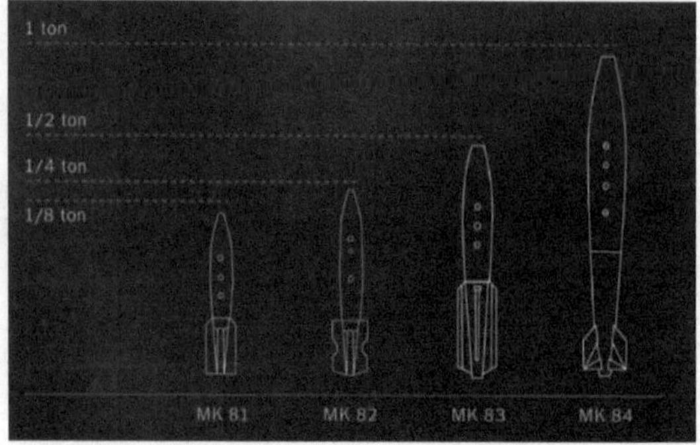

Source: New York Times (2017)

Figure 13: RWM Italia share of MK 80 license revenues

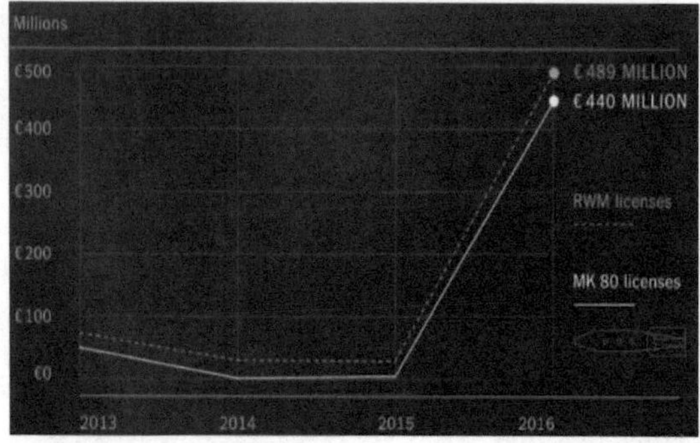

Source: New York Times (2017)

As a result of its multi-domestic strategy, the Rheinmetall Group has a very diverse product portfolio that is adapted to the specific customers i.e. the governments in the countries of operation. The product portfolio ranges from hand grenades to grenade and mortar ammunition, shells for rapid-fire cannons and naval

---

88 The annual reports of RWM Italia for the years 2015 show that RWM Italia 72% of its turnover € 48.1 million with unguided and guided aircraft bombs. Saudi Arabia accounted for 55% in 2015. The UAE for 15%. Thus, more than two thirds of RWM Italia's sales were generated with two countries that were at war in Yemen.

89 The German RDM Managing Director, Norbert Schulz, called the commitment in South Africa "the best business decision Rheinmetall has made in the last 20 years" (Nassauer 2018, 41).

guns to artillery and tank grenades as well as bombs for aircraft. Many of these products are produced at several of the plants with only slight variations.

Rheinmetall pursues its goal of "internationalisation" in several ways. Firstly, the group has vertically integrated suppliers. This means it has bought and modernised ammunition manufacturers abroad to expand its product portfolio. Most notably, in 2007 Rheinmetall acquired the Swiss fuse specialist Zaugg Elektronik AG, significantly expanding its portfolio of fuses. In this way the Group was able to produce its ammunitions more independently, without having to rely on expensive external supplies of fuses (Nassauer 2016). Secondly, the group diversifies horizontally by buying companies in other countries to get access to their markets and products[90]. Thirdly, the Group supplies customers in third countries with production facilities through its subsidiaries and joint ventures abroad.

For instance, on 27th March 2016 a delegation of the Rheinmetall/Denel joint venture, together with South African President Jacob Zuma inaugurated an ammunition plant in the Saudi town Al Kharj. Such production facilities are either organised and operated as joint ventures between the Rheinmetall companies and local firms or handed over to local partners ready for use and then supplied with components and technical services from the Rheinmetall Group (Nassauer 2018). Direct exports are a more lucrative business, however, "Rheinmetall customers are increasingly interested in establishing part of the value chain in their country" which requires sellers to adapt their sales strategies by offering offsets (B-I-2). It is important to note that Rheinmetall trades goods with customers whose supply would not be authorised from Germany directly. Often the customer can choose whether the ammunition of the desired type is to be supplied from German, European or non-European production. For the group it makes little difference from where the sale is conducted as no matter where the profits are generated, they flow back into the Group's coffers (Ger-NGO-2). Furthermore, due to the fact that Rheinmetall supplies Saudi Arabia from both Italy and South Africa, the company is less vulnerable to policy changes in one country.

Figure 14:
Opening of SAMI Ammunition Factory
Source: Saudi Government (2016)

90 Most recently, Rheinmetall has announced plans to buy the land vehicle arm of BAE Systems as well as the French/German KNDS. This would give the company access to the British and French market (Sprenger 2018)

In the aftermath of the RWM Italia bomb sales to Saudi Arabia coupled with the murder of Jamal Khashoggi, there has been fierce discussion in Italy to ban arms sales to Saudi Arabia. Nonetheless, even if the Italian government decided to take a more restrictive stance, Rheinmetall would still be able to ship a large amount of ammunition supplies from the South African Denel Plant or from other subsidiaries. The annual report of 2019 states that Rheinmetall will continue its internationalisation through M&A strategies, however, due to the prospect of rising military spending in Germany and other NATO states it is expected that more sales will be made on the German home market in the near future (27).

11.2 Rheinmetall Relations with the German Government

While the example of Heckler and Koch showed how companies pursue non-market strategies to improve ties with the home government, Rheinmetall provides a different example. In recent years, company officials have often issued warnings to the German government that the low level of military spending coupled with the strict German export laws will lead to a loss of jobs and expertise in the defence sector.

The extent to which Rheinmetall aims to be independent of the German market is illustrated by comments of Dr Andreas Schwer (2013), former CEO of Zurich-based Rheinmetall International Holding AG. In an interview about a potential joint venture with Turkish MKEK, Schwer said "the idea is to come [to Turkey] and develop their own ammunition with them, free of German technology rights. We want to make Turkey independent of foreign suppliers and support Turkey in its intention to become self-sufficient by 2023" (9). The aim was to build up local development and production capacities "based on Turkish technology rights" in order to avoid German export restrictions (ibid.). Similarly, Armin Papperberger, CEO of Rheinmetall stated that due to overly strong arms regulations in Germany the new seal of quality was "German Free" instead of "Made in Germany" and that therefore more and more production plants will be moved abroad (Bickel 2017, 24).

The ambiguous stance of the German government towards the company was illustrated in several interviews. On the one hand, government civil servants voiced strong criticism over the company's conduct abroad (US-FO-1). On the other hand, the importance of companies such as Rheinmetall for maintaining a German Defence Industrial Base was emphasised (US-BW-2). In addition, the embargo to Saudi Arabia has caused conflict, as the company threatened to take the government to court for failure to act. Nevertheless, the government has supported the company's international endeavours on several occasions, for instance in 2012, when Sigmar Gabriel convinced the Indian government to take the Swiss Rheinmetall subsidiary off its black list where it had been relegated due to corruption allegations (Zeit 2018).

Finally, it is worth pausing to consider that even though Rheinmetall's actions on the international plain often undermine Germany's arms export policy, the German state indirectly benefits from this, as a number of German financial firms and retirement funds are shareholders of the company and therefore profit from revenues the company generates by circumventing German export restrictions (Grüll & Hoffman 2018). The following section seeks to find out what policies the German government has put in place to prevent the supply of pariah states via affiliated companies or joint ventures abroad.

11.3 Government Stance and Policy

As indicated at the beginning of this chapter, the German government cannot legally intervene in deals between the Rheinmetall affiliates abroad and other governments, unless the trade involves German technology rights for which an end-use declaration has been signed. Moreover, as the example with HK has shown – even if re-export agreements are signed, they can be ignored and the diversion resulting from this can hardly be investigated or enforced legally. Nonetheless, in the optimal case where an end-use declaration is not broken and the exporting country consults the German government, the risk of unwanted technology transfer is low. This is the angle that government officials highlighted in interviews to reassure the secure functioning of the export regime (US-FO-2).

However, for this case it is useful to take a slightly different angle, as Rheinmetall does not *per se* trans-ship German technology illegally from its plants abroad. Instead, the company (1) researches and develops new products that are very similar to the German counterparts (2) produces weapons under license such as the MK 80 bombs (3) or buys up foreign firms to benefit from the existing technology rights (UK-NGO-1). An example of how this is done provides the RDM joint venture where Rheinmetall is the main shareholder. Herein, the company benefits from technology that South Africa developed on its own accord as a result of being embargoed during the Apartheid regime (Ger-NGO-1). However, despite the fact that there appear to be no German technology rights involved, these strategies pose a threat to German foreign policy. This is because the company uses the know-how it received from German government investments in order to equip Third States with armament goods and production facilities. Such strategies are possible due to a lack of regulatory measures.

11.4 Technical Assistance and the Export of Data

The control of the export of data has become more and more difficult as a result of technological evolution. As an illustration, sending an email to a foreign buyer that contains information on the specifics of a certain defence product is illegal, if no prior license has been granted. Nowadays, control officials face great challenges as large amounts of data can be stored on small hard drives which are difficult to detect by standard border control practices. In addition, data within companies is shared via online clouds, for example, which can be accessed from any place that provides internet access (Commission 2015, 98). The engineers abroad can then build from previous plans and alter the product slightly and thereby avoid intellectual property and export control regulations, an illegal practice that is difficult to detect or investigate. In addition to the control of data and plans, the issue of regulating technical assistance and services is becoming increasingly important.

While the transfer of technical data in all its forms (plans, models, drafts etc.) is subject to licensing, providing technical assistance to foreign companies without data transfer is less restricted. Such technical assistance can take several forms including teaching, training, work support or counselling services (B-EU-1). In order to be exempted from a license the person providing the service must, however not export any material information when leaving the country. Technical assistance provides several risks of proliferation and diversion, even without the export of data, as engineers can help assemble existing production lines or ammunition filling stations in foreign countries. As a matter of fact, such services are especially important to Third States like Saudi Arabia or Turkey, who currently rely on foreign engineers in order to build their own technological industrial base. At present, the regulation that would prevent companies like Rheinmetall from sending their personnel all over the world to help researching or developing armaments is very limited, especially when the services are provided via an affiliate company abroad. Under German law technical assistance is only subject to a licensing requirement in certain instances, such as if it is related to:

1)the production or development of NBC weapons or missiles that could carry such weapons, if the customer is located in a Third State (§49 AWV)

2)a military-end use in countries subject to an EU, OSCE, UNSC arms embargo (§50 AWV)

3)the construction and operation of facilities for nuclear purposes (§52 AWV)

4)listed goods of communication surveillance in Third States (§52 a,b, AWV)

Unless the above restrictions apply, any German citizen is free to contribute to military projects in Third States[91]. The second legal restriction is especially relevant for this case study, that is, to restrict only technical assistance with a military purpose to countries that are subject to an institutionalised arms embargo. This raises a number of issues. Firstly, the decision to stop arms sales to Saudi Arabia is neither an institutionalised embargo under the EU, OSCE or UN, nor is it a legally binding national embargo. Instead, the government has merely politically decided to put export decisions on halt. This means that under the current circumstances German citizens can continue to service Saudi ammunition filling stations or the G36 production line. In that sense, the foreign policy gets undermined as direct exports are forbidden but services to help produce armaments in the country are not preventable. This condition does not only severely limit the German government's ability to effectively implement embargos, but it also makes it impossible to prevent German engineers from supporting autocratic regimes in their efforts to establish a military industrial base.

In frameworks of other countries, such as the United States, technical assistance is regulated more restrictively. In the US system any citizen needs authorisation to assist in services related to military purposes, irrespective of whether there is an embargo or not[92]. If the German government had a similar regulation in place most services with a military purpose that a German national provides anywhere on earth would require prior authorisation. One way of implementing such a law would be to expand the license requirement for technical assistance with a military purpose to all Third States, and not only in instances when embargos have been applied. Such a regulation would pose obstacles for transnational companies to freely trade and service armament factories all over the globe. Finally, it would allow the German government to prevent pariah states from establishing a military industrial base that is rooted in products that are closely related to German technology.

11.5 Exerting Political Pressure

Given the limited legal ways to intervene in exports from abroad that do not contain German technology but are carried out by German firms and German citizens, the question arises whether there is a political interest to intervene in such trade strategies. Based on the idea that 25% of Rheinmetall's revenues come from the German home market and that the majority of R&D investments are provided by

[91] The EU Joint Action on Regulating Technical Assistance (2000/401/CFSP) does not contain additional regulatory controls either and is not implemented by many Member States (Commission 2015, 88).

[92] US Code §124.1. "The requirements [to obtain approval for defence services] apply whether or not technical data is to be disclosed or used in the performance of the defense services described in §120.9 (e-CFR 2019)."

the Federal State, one might imagine that the government has the power to pressure the company into refraining from such sales strategies abroad. On this matter, the interviews have left a mixed impression.

On the one hand, it became clear that the government indeed exerts a certain level of influence over its defence companies, if it detects controversial or morally impermissible sales actions. As a member of the Foreign Office put it, "if we tell the company to take a look at a certain issue, they normally do so and problems get resolved without needing to resort to legal action" (US-FO-1). As these lines of communications are shielded from the public it is difficult to assess how often this takes place and under what conditions. However, the interviews also conveyed the idea that such interactions are mainly limited to Rheinmetall's engagements related to the German government and not with regards to activities of its affiliates or joint ventures abroad (ibid.). Questions as to whether it raises concerns that the actions of German-owned firms located abroad severely undermine German foreign-policy were blocked with the argument that these companies are legally-speaking not under German jurisdiction and that therefore the German authorities´ hands were tied (US-BW-1).

The empirical evidence shows no interventions have been made in controversial ammunition deals. This validates the assumption that the German Federal Government does not have the political will or power to solve these issues via informal communication channels.

In countries like France or Switzerland this is different. An example is provided by the Swiss RUAG Simulation Company LLC in Abu Dhabi, which is an affiliated of Ruag Swiss P and which stopped trading with Saudi Arabia as result of the Yemen conflict. The Swiss government issued a statement saying that this plant will no longer deal with Saudi Arabia, as affiliated companies must not provide a means of circumventing Swiss arms regulations (RUAG Group 2016). It is important to note though that this was not a legal or a political decision, but is to be seen as a business decision that the government was able to take because of its influence as a shareholder. In France and the UK but Switzerland in particular, governments hold "golden shares" in many of their national defence companies, which allows the government to function as an oversight committee. Consequently, they can directly influence business decisions, such as influencing certain sales operations or electing board members of the defence company (James 2019).

Given that the German government has completely privatised its defence and therefore is unable to intervene once a subsidiary is established, the question arises of whether there is a way to prevent the establishment of affiliated companies abroad when there is reason to believe that the cooperation with autocratic governments would lead to undermining export practices. Civil servant interviewees repeatedly referred to the fact that this is legally impossible (US-FO-1;2). Firstly, as stated above under the Foreign Payments Act, business have the right to foreign trade which can only be withdrawn in very limited cases (cf. chapter 7.2). However, looking at the costs and benefits of having transnational defence firms, it appears that costs of not being able to establish a coherent arms export and foreign policy are lower than the economic and political benefits for governments.

In fact, the government has an interest in allowing its national defence companies to access foreign markets as this reduces the amount of money necessary to keep large defence contractors alive. This is based on the rationale that preventing internationalisation strategies while at the same time reducing military expenditure would eventually put an end to German defence firms, which in turn poses a risk to national security. In addition, a strong presence of companies in foreign markets indirectly generates political capital and foreign policy influence. The Rheinmetall M&A strategies in Italy and South Africa did not only prevent the local factories from going out of business but it also created jobs in the local area and revenues for the municipalities which now depend on the presence and investments of the German company.

Arguably, this also increases the power of the German state, not at least because it benefits from the profits that flow back into Germany. In addition, the German defence technological industrial base (DTIB) benefits from getting access to foreign technology rights, which can be easily transferred when a local company is bought by a foreign firm (US-FO-3). Therefore, there are several political and economic reasons that argue against influencing the global activities of Rheinmetall even if they undermine German foreign policy principles.

11.6 Evaluation: Affiliated Companies and Joint Ventures Abroad

The study of the Rheinmetall market structure and business conduct in relation to the German policy framework shows that the German government currently has limited means to interfere with the trade activities of Rheinmetall abroad when no German technology right is involved. This is primarily due to the global structure of the company that allows it to transfer production to countries with less stringent export policies. Specifically, the study of the regulation of technical assistance shows that the German government has room to manoeuvre to control trade activities abroad more strictly.

In the context of the recent announcements of the Saudi and Turkish government to become independent producers of weapon technology, this poses several risks, not only due to the problematic human rights situation in these countries but also with regard to their aggressive foreign policy on neighbouring states. It is questionable whether the German government has an interest in allowing its companies to contribute to the defence-industrial independence of these countries in the long term[93].

11.7 Theorising Affiliated Companies and Joint Ventures Abroad

It appears that leaving the internationalisation strategies of national companies unrestricted, is largely based on an economic liberal premise while also pertaining to realist notions of power expansion. Leaving national companies abroad unrestricted, Germany is able to lower its military expenditure but simultaneously preserve its power and increase its foreign-policy influence by having companies access foreign markets. This safeguards the national defence industrial base which Germany needs "to participate as an equal partner in the shaping and implementation of armaments cooperation within the framework of the European security and defence policy" (Federal Government 2004, 5).

A significant political side-effect is that the human rights issues caused by German companies abroad are not directly attributable to the German government as they only rarely enter the national public sphere and are thus, seemingly, beyond the national jurisdiction. From a neo-realist point of view the only concern that this could raise is related to the fact that renouncing extraterritorial measures to control defence trade can pose national security threats. Hence some measures have been put in place for the most relevant security aspects, such as those related to the production of nuclear arms or surveillance technology.

It is also worth noting that applying national law extraterritorially, to the detriment of other states, requires an elevated position in the international system. Arguably, the USA is able to implement strong extraterritorial measures because its position in the international system allows it to do so without having to fear serious opposition. Nevertheless, in the German case it appears that security and human rights considerations are traded for economic benefits and foreign policy influence. As long as no goods and services are traded that pose a direct threat to German national security it is a win-win situation, as the Italian and South African State benefit from employment and export profits that could not be achieved without the help of a foreign company that possesses the necessary know-how and financial resources. Finally, from the view of the citizens in the countries that suffer from exports to autocratic regimes such as the families in Yemen, this must be seen as a mercantilist approach where economic superiority is used to augment state power at the expense of other countries.

93 In 2017 the Royal family established the Saudi Arabian Military Industries (SAMI) with the goal to "achieve the Kingdom's self-sufficiency in military industries" and to be "among the top 25 military industry companies in the world by 2030" (https://www.sami.com.sa/).

12.0 Conclusion and Outlook

This research has found that, by and large, states are still capable of controlling licit arms trade, if they so wish. However, globalisation dynamics have created a system in which European states find themselves under increasing systemic pressure to coordinate and possibly compromise their national controls. This has happened mainly for two reasons: Firstly, changes in the power dynamics of the defence market have created an increased dependency on buyer states. Secondly, the inflation of costs in producing military equipment have forced exporting countries to move towards market liberalization and respectively deregulation.

Indications of hyper-globalisation - or what Ann Markusen (1990) called the "rise of the world weapons" – were only found during the study of dual-use trade in the EU, as well as during the analysis of regulation concerning trade of conventional arms and related services by German affiliated companies outside the EU. When it comes to dual-use trade, hyper-globalisation took place because EU countries have decided to deregulate internal trade while not fully harmonising external trade controls. In the case of the trade of activities of nationally rooted companies abroad (affiliates), it was shown that hyper-globalization exists mainly due to a lack of extraterritorial control measures. In sum, the lack of coordination among states, coupled with the difficulties to monitor the trade of certain technologies and related services, can allow transnational companies to export from countries with weaker regulations. Nonetheless, the evidence of other control regimes, such as that of the US or Switzerland, suggests that extraterritorial trade could be controlled to a much greater extent. Yet this would require a partial nationalization of defence firms or to impose extraterritorial controls on other sovereign states.

In this context, Pearstein's (2011) idea that "the extent of the market is limited by the workable scope of its regulation" needs to be refined. In the case of arms exports, the extent of the market depends on the normative self-conception of a state and on whether the state's position in the international system allows it to enforce control principles extraterritorially. Given that Germany considers itself a "globally networked country that due to its economic, political and military significance has a strong responsibility to play an active role in shaping global order", there is reason to believe that it has willingly decided to sacrifice certain control principles for economic and alliance interests (White Paper 2016, 72).

In fact, this study has yielded more detailed insights into how states with a strong defence industry balance economic liberalisation with neo-realist rationales. Moreover, the theoretical reflections give reason to think that no single IR paradigm or economic philosophy is able to explain the functioning of the German arms exports control regimes and its underlying principles in its entirety. Instead an argument for eclectic and interdisciplinary approaches to the matter has been made. Therein, economic liberalist thinking was strongly reflected in instances where goods or services with low relevance for the national industrial base were traded with close allies. Most notably this is illustrated by the Eurofighter cooperation where the trade of most components is loosely regulated, whereas the export of the final product is a sovereign decision. The inference that can be drawn is that the more relevant a good is to the preservation of the national defence industrial base, the more neo-realist thinking takes over and the more national prerogatives are asserted.

The second case study then expanded this reasoning by showing that economic liberalisation becomes less dominant when it comes to goods that cause a large number of casualties, such as small arms. Here, the positivist assumptions about power maximisation are unable to explain why Germany has consciously decided to weaken its dominant position in the small-arms market. Instead of materialist ideas on power politics, the export regime has been influenced by social constructions of norms that are traceable to NGO campaigning. Yet, since several of these small arms control measures are still quite new and there are already indicators of a lack of political will to implement them, it remains to be seen whether the normative constructions will be able to overcome long-established self-help thinking. Finally, a prediction can be made regarding the future regulation of extraterritorial trade:

If the goods and services that German engineers provide to Third States lead to the development of technologies that threaten the German defence industrial base, it is likely that stricter extraterritorial measures will be introduced. However, this would require, first, that Germany maintains its elevated role in the international system and, second, that core actors in German society pay closer attention to the issues caused by such business strategies, leading to a change of the legal system.

While this work has focussed on the external dimension of export control, future research may look at whether national control systems are well-adapted to challenges related to increasing foreign-direct investments (FDIs) in the domestic defence industry, from China for instance. Furthermore, future works may look more closely at the factors that influence decision making in the arms export control domain and explore the briefly outlined theoretical perspectives in more depth Such works may draw from the findings of this research which serves to illustrate that the study of arms exports controls can yield fruitful insights into the central dynamics that govern the politico-economic relations between states.

13.0 Bibliography

Alves, Péricles Gasparini. 1992. "Access to outer space technologies: implications for international security." Vol. 15. United Nations Publications.

Amnesty International. 2017. "Geneva: As global arms trade surges, states greenlight reckless, harmful deals." https://www.amnesty.org/en/latest/news/2017/09/geneva-as-global-arms-trade-surges-states greenlight-reckless-harmful-deals/

Assemblée Nationale. 2000. *Rapport d'information sur le contrôle des exportations d'armement.* Présenté par Jean-Claude Sandrier, Christian Martin et Alain Veyret, Députés. No. 2334. Paris, 25 Avril, 2000.

Baldwin, Richard, and Philippe Martin.1999. "Two waves of globalisation: superficial similarities,fundamental differences." *National Bureau of Economic Research,* 01 January, 1999.

Balsiger, Jörg.2019. *Logic of appropriateness.* Encyclopaedia Britannica. 2019. https://www.britannica.com/topic/logic-of-appropriateness

Basic Law for the Federal Republic of Germany, 23 May, 1949.

Bellais, Renaud, and Susan Jackson. 2014. "Defence Firms beyond National Borders: Internationalisation or Multi-Domestic Approach?. " In *The evolving boundaries of defence: an assessment of recent shifts in defence activities*, 231-249. Emerald Group Publishing.

Béraud-Sudreau .2014. "French adaptation strategies for arms export controls since the 1990s." Paris *Paper* no. 10. Strategic Research Institute of the French Military Academy (IRSEM).

Bickel, Markus. 2017. *Die Profiteure des Terrors wie Deutschland an Kriegen verdient und arabische Diktaturen stärkt.* Westend Verlag.

Bickerton, Christopher, Dermot Hodson, and Uwe Puetter. 2015. "The New Intergovernmentalism: European Integration in the Post-Maastricht Era". *Journal of Common Market Studies*,*53*(4): 703-722.

Bitzinger, Richard. 1994. "The globalization of the arms industry: The next proliferation challenge." *International Security* 19, no. 2 170-198.

Bode, Hans- Günter, and Heinz Gläser. 1978. *Rüstung in der Bundesrepublik Deutschland*. Regensburg: Walhalla & Praetoria.

Bomben für die Welt. 2018. Directed by Philipp Grüll and Karl Hoffman. ARD. Germany. 2018.

Bröker, Anja, and Christian Thiels. 2018. "Eurofighter für Katar - Deutschland macht mit." Tageschau. https://www.tagesschau.de/inland/eurofighter-katar-101.html

Bromley, Mark, and Hugh Griffiths. 2010. "End-user certificates: improving standards to prevent diversion". *SIPRI*, no. 2010/3.

Bromley, Mark. 2012. "The Review of the EU Common Position on Arms Exports: Prospects for Strengthened Control". EU Non-Proliferation Consortium.

Bromley, Mark., Neil Cooper, and Paul Holtom. 2012. "The UN Arms Trade Treaty: arms export controls, the human security agenda and the lessons of history". *International Affairs 88*(5): 1029-1048.

Brooks, Stephen. 2005. *Producing Security: Multinational Corporations, Globalization, and the changing of conflict*. Princeton University Press.

Brüggemann, Michael, and Hartmut Wessler. 2012. *Transnationale Kommunikation. Eine Einführung*. Springer-Verlag.

Bryman, Alan. 2016. *Social Research Methods*. Oxford University Press.

Brzoska, Michael, and Hartmut Küchle. "Folgen, Auswirkungen und Gestaltungsmöglichkeiten internationaler Abkommen für eine restriktive deutsche Rüstungsexportpolitik." BICC, 2002.

Bundesamt für Wirtschaft und Ausfuhrkontrolle BAFA. 2017. "Endverbleibs-dokumente - Erläuterungenzur praktischen Verwendung von Endverbleibs-dokumenten". August 2017.

Bundeszentrale für politische Bildung (BpB) 2012. "Fallstudie Kleinwaffen in Deutschland".

Coalition Treaty. 2018. "Ein neuer Aufbruch für Europa, Eine neue Dynamik für Deutschland, Ein neuer Zusammenhalt für unser Land. Koalitionsvertrag zwischen CDU, CSU und SPD." 12 March, 2018.

Cops, Diederik, Nils Duquet, and Gregory Gourdin. 2017. *Towards Europeanised arms export controls.Comparing control systems in EU Member States*. Flemish Peace Institute. Artoos.

Council Common Position 2008/944/CFSP of 8 December 2008 defining common rules governing control of exports of military technology and equipment, *Official Journal of the European Union*, L335, 08 December 2008.

Davis, Ian. 2002.*The Regulation of Arms and Dual-Use Exports; Germany, Sweden and the UK*. PhD diss. Oxford. University Press.

DeVore, Marc. 2013. "Arms production in the global village: Options for adapting to defense-industrial globalization." *Security studies* 22, 532-572.

Eavis, Paul. and Shannon A. 1994. "Arms and dual-use export controls: priorities for the European Union." *Saferworld* Briefing, London, June 1994.

Elman, Colin. 1996. "Horses for courses: Why nor neorealist theories of foreign policy?". *Security Studies* 6: 7-53.

European Commission. 2015. *Final Report: Data and information collection for EU dual use export control policy review*. Written by SIPRI and Ecorys. Brussels 06 November, 2015.

European Commission. 2016. *Impact Assessment. Report on the EU Export Control Policy Review*. Brussels: 28 September 2016.

European Commission. 2018. Impact Assessment. Proposal for a Regulation establishing the European Defence Fund. Brussels, 13 June 2018.

European Council. 2000. "Joint Action concerning the control of technical assistance related to certain military end-uses." 2000/401/CFSP. *Official Journal of the European Communities*, L159, 30 June 2000: 216-217.

European Council. 2008. "Common Position 2008/944/CFSP of 08 December 2008 defining common rules governing control of exports of military technology and equipment".

European Council. 2009. "Regulation (EC) No 428/2009 of 5 May 2009 setting up a Community regime for the control of exports, transfer, brokering and transit of dual-use items".

European Council. 2018. "Nineteenth Annual Report according to Article 8(2) of Council Common Position 2008/944/CFSP defining common rules governing the control of exports of military technology and equipment." *Official Journal of the European Union.* 14 February, 2018.

European Parliament. 2018. "Draft Report on the Council's annual report in accordance with Operative Provision 8 of the European Union Code of Conduct on Arms Exports." *Committee on Foreign Affairs.* 29 June, 2018.

European Parliamentary Research Service Blog. 2015. "EU Rules on Control of Arms Exports." 14 December, 2015. https://epthinktank.eu/2015/12/14/eu-rules-on-control-of-arms-exports/.

European Union, *Consolidated version of the Treaty on the Functioning of the European Union*, 13 December, 2007/C 115/01.

European Union, *Treaty Establishing the European Community (Consolidated Version), Rome Treaty*. 25 March, 1957.

European Union, *Treaty on the European Union (Consolidated Version), Treaty of Maastricht*, 7 February 1992, Official Journal of the European Communities 325/5. 24 December, 2002.

Export Manager. 2018. North-America. Frankfurt Business Media. Edition 9. 14, November 2018.

Farnborough Agreement. 2000. "Framework Agreement between The French Republic, The Federal Republic of Germany, The Italian Republic, The Kingdom of Spain, The Kingdom of Sweden and The United Kingdom of Great Britain and Northern Ireland Concerning Measures to Facilitate the Restructuring and Operation of the European Defence Industry." Farnborough Air Show, 27 July, 2000.

Federal Government. 2004. Antwort auf die Kleine Anfrage der Abgeordneten Erich G.Fritz u.a. Drucksache 15/2363. Berlin. 15 January, 2004.

Federal Government. 2010. "Waffenexporte - Kontrolle des Endverbleibs deutscher Kriegswaffen und Rüstungsgüter." Drucksache 17/3861. Deutscher Bundestag, 23 November, 2010.

Federal Government. 2010. Antwort auf Kleine Anfrage von Jan Van Aken, Christine Buchholz, Dr. Diether Dehm. "Waffenexporte - Kontrolle des Endverbleibs deutscher Kriegswaffen und Rüstungsgüter." Drucksache 17/3861. 23 November. 2010.

Federal Government. 2015. "Rüstungsexportentscheidungen des Bundes-sicherheitsrates." Drucksache 18/4194. Deutscher Bundestag, 04 March, 2015.

Federal Government. 2015. Antwort auf die Kleine Anfrage von Jan van Aken, Christine Buchholz, Annette Groth und der Fraktion DIE LINKE."Fusion von Krauss-Maffei Wegmann und Nexter." Drucksache 18/5511. 08 July, 2015.

Federal Government. 2015. *Strategy Paper of the Federal Government on Strengthening the Defence Industry in Germany*. Berlin, 21 July, 2015.

Federal Government. 2016. Antwort auf die Kleine Anfrage von Jan van Aken. "Genehmigungen für den Rüstungsexport nach Saudi-Arabien im zweiten Halbjahr 2015." Drucksache18/7274. 15 January, 2016.

Federal Ministry for Economic Affairs and Energy. 2018."A restrictive, responsible policy on the export of military equipment."

Federal Ministry For Economic Affairs and Energy. 2019. "Principles of the German Federal Government governing the export of small arms and light weapons, corresponding ammunition and production equipment to third countries." ("Small Arm Principles") 29 May, 2015.

Federal Ministry of Defence. 2016. "White Paper On German Security Policy and the Future of the Bundeswehr." Berlin, 13 July 2016.

Foreign Relations. 2018. [Electronic] US Code of Federal Regulations, title 22. 28 March, 2019.

Foreign Trade and Payments Act of 6 June 2013 (Federal Law Gazette I p. 1482), as last amended by Article 4 of the Act of 20 July 2017 (Federal Law Gazette I p. 2789).

Foreign Trade and Payments Ordinance of 02 August 2013 (Federal Law Gazette [BGBl.] Part I p. 2865), as last amended by Article 1 of the Ordinance of 19 December, 2018.

Friederichs, Hauke. 2014. "Die Sünden der deutschen Rüstungsexporte." *Zeit Online*, 2 June, 2014. https://www.zeit.de/politik/deutschland/2014-06/ruestung-waffen-export

Friederichs, Hauke. 2017. "Heckler & Koch: Gewinner des Jahres." *Zeit Online*, 11 December, 2017. https://www.zeit.de/2017/51/heckler-koch-waffen-waffenexporte-umsatz

Gabelnick, Tamar, and Anna Rich. 2000. "Globalized weaponry." *Social Justice* 27.4 (82 (2000): 37-44.

Gebauer, Matthias. 2015a. "Deutsche Gewehre im Jemen: Bundesregierung gibt Lücke bei Waffenexport-Kontrolle zu." *Spiegel Online,* 12 June, 2015.

———.2015b. "Kampf gegen den IS: Deutscher Waffen-Nachschub für die Peschmerga." *Spiegel Online* 18 December, 2015.

———. 2016. "Urteil im Fall Heckler & Koch: Regierung muss über Waffenexport nach Saudi-Arabien entscheiden." *Spiegel Online*, 23 June, 2016.

Grässlin, Jürgen. 2013. *Schwarzbuch Waffenhandel: Wie Deutschland Am Krieg Verdient*. Heyne Verlag.

Griffiths, Philip. 2018. "The Wassenaar Arrangement: Transparency and Effectiveness in Regulating Transfers of Conventional Arms and Dual-Use Goods and Technologies." *International Seminar on strategic Export Controls.* Islamabad 09 May, 2018.

Guay, Terrence. 2009. "Globalization and the Transatlantic Defense Industrial Base." *UNISCI Discussion Papers* no. 19 (January): 86-109.

H&K AG. 2018. "Consolidated financial statements as of 31 December 2017 and Group management report." https://www.heckler-koch.com/de/ir/abschluesse.html.

Handelsbatt. 2018."Rheinmetall exportiert weiter Waffen nach Saudi-Arabien." *12* December, 2018.

Hansen, Susanne Therese. 2016. "Taking ambiguity seriously: Explaining the indeterminacy of the European Union conventional arms export control regime". *European Journal of International Relations*, 22(1): 192-216.

Harnisch, Sebastian, and Hanns Maull. 2001. *Germany as a civilian power? The foreign policy of the Berlin Republic*. Manchester University Press.

Hauge, Rod, Martin Harrop, and Shaun Breslin. 2016. *Comparative Government and Politics: An Introduction*. 10th Edition. MacMillan.

Herby, Peter. 1999. "Arms availability and the situation of civilians in armed conflict - Summary of an ICRC study for the 27th International Conference of the Red Cross and Red Crescent". *Revue Internationale de la Croix-Rouge/International Review of the Red Cross* 81, no. 835: 669-672. doi:10.1017/S1560775500059861.

Holtom, Paul and Irene Pavesi. 2017. "Trade Update 2017-Out of the Shadows." *Small Arm Survey*, 2017.http://www.smallarmssurvey.org/fileadmin/docs/S-Trade-Update/SAS-Trade-Update-2017.

How did bombs made in Italy kill a family in Yemen?. 2017. Directed by Malachy Browne and Barbara Marcolini. The New York Times. 29 December, 2017.

James, Andrew. 2002. "Comparing European responses to defence industry globalization." *Defence & security analysis* 18, 123-143.

James, Andrew. 2019. "EU and US revenues in home and international market by Frost and Sullivan 2014." *The Political Economy of the Defence Industry*. Sciences Po Paris, 12 March, 2019.

Joint Conference Church and Development GKKE. 2017. Arms Export Report presented by the GKKE Working group on Arms Exports. 18 December, 2017.

Joyner, Daniel. 2017. Non-proliferation export controls: origins, challenges, and proposals for strengthening. Ashgate Publishing.

Karp, Aaron. 2018. "Estimating global Civilian-held firearms numbers." *Small Arms Survey*, 2017.

Katzenstein, Peter. 2010. Beyond Paradigms: Analytic Eclecticism in the Study of World Politics. Palgrave.

Kimball, Daryl. 2017. “Fact Sheets & Briefs The Wassenaar Arrangement at a Glance.” *Arms Control Association*, 11 December, 2017.

Knight, Ben. 2017. Deutsche Welle: “UN’S Arms Trade Treaty `too weak to make a difference´.”

Knöpfle, Claudia. 2017. “Endverbleibskontrolle exportierter Waffen hat begonnen.” *Bayrischer Rund-funk*, 30 August, 2017.

Kollewe, Julia. 2017. “BAE Systems to cut nearly 2,000 UK jobs.” *The Guardian*, 10 October, 2017.

Küchle, Hartmut. 2005. *Die Neustrukturierung des deutschen Rüstungsmarktes als industriepolitische Aufgabe*. Düsseldorf: Hans-Böckler-Stiftung. [Restructuring the German defence market as an industrial policy task].

Lagneau, Laurent. 2014. “À nouveau, Berlin bloque l’exportation de matériels militaires francais.” *Zone militaire*. 14 September, 2014.

Lequesne, Christian. 2015. “EU foreign policy through the lens of practice theory: A different approach to the European External Action Service.” Cooperation and conflict 50, no. 3 (2015): 351-367.

Markowski, Stefan, and Robert Wylie. 2007. “The emergence of European defence and defence Industry policies.” *Security Challenges 3 (2)*: 31-51.

Markusen, Ann, and Sean Costigan, eds. 1999. “Arming the Future: A defense industry for the 21st century”. Council on Foreign Relations Press.

Markusen, Ann. 1999. "The rise of world weapons". *Foreign Policy*, no. 114 (spring): 40-51.

Meijer, Hugo. 2014. “Transatlantic Perspectives on China’s Military Modernization: The Case of Europe’s Arms Embargo against the People’s Republic of China.” *Paris Paper* no. 12. Strategic Research Institute of the French Military Academy (IRSEM).

———.2016. *Trading with the Enemy - The Making of US Export Control Policy toward the People's Republic of China.* Oxford University Press.

———. 2018. *The Handbook of European Defence Policies and Armed Forces.* Oxford University Press.

Moltmann, Bernhard. 2012. "Die Zange, die nicht kneift: der EU-Gemeinsame Standpunkt zu Rüstungsexporten-Chancen und Risiken seiner Überprüfung." HSFK Report no.3/2012.

Monreal, Christoph, and Hermann Runte. 2000. "Das aktuelle Exportkontrollrecht - Ein Überblick." GewArch, 142-148.

Moravcsik, Andrew. 1991. "Arms and autarky in modern European history." *Daedalus* 23-45.

———. 1997. "Taking preferences seriously: A liberal theory of international politics." *International Organization* 51.4 (1997): 513-553.

Nassauer, Otfried, and Christopher Steinmetz. 2005. "*Made in Germany" inside - Komponenten – die vergessenen Rüstungsexporte*. Studie in Kooperation von Oxfam Deutschland und dem Berliner Informationszentrum für Transatlantische Sicherherheit.

Nassauer, Otfried .2016. "Hemmungslos und unersättlich - Rheinmetall und die Munitionsexporte."*Berliner Informationszentrum für Transatlantische Sicherheit,* 2016. https://www.bits.de/public/unv_a/orginal-041116.htm#fn1

———. 2018. "Munitionsgeschäfte in deutscher Verantwortung EXPLOSIV, TÖDLICH und PROFITABEL." *Evangelische Landeskirche in Baden und Berliner Informationszentrum für Transatlantische Sicherheit,* 2018. http://www.bits.de/public/pdf/rr18-01.pdf.

Nye, Joseph S. 1988. „Neorealism and Neoliberalism." *World Politics* 40: 235-251.

Organisation for Security and Cooperation in Europe. 2003. *Best practice guide on export control of small arms and light weapons.* Vienna: OSCE Secretariat.

Organisation for Security and Cooperation in Europe. 2012. "Document on Small Arms and Light Weapons." 308th Plenary Meeting of the OSCE Forum for Security Cooperation on 24 November, 2000. https://www.osce.org/fsc/20783.

Pauly, Marcel, and Vanessa Steinmetz. 2018. "Rüstungsexporte: Deutschlands Geschäft mit dem Krieg". *Spiegel Online,* 02 January 2018. http://www.spiegel.de/politik/ausland/ruestungs exporte-so-steht-es-um-die-branche-in-deutschland-a-1189627.html.

Pearlstein, Steven. 2011. "Dani Rodrik's `The Globalization Paradox´." *Washington Post*, 13 March, 2011.

Platte, Hendrik, and Dirk Leuffen. 2016. "German arms exports: between normative aspirations and political reality." *German politics* 25.4 (2016): 561-580.

Political Principles of the Federal Government for the Export of Weapons of War and Other Military Equipment, Presse- und Informationsamt der Bundesregierung, no. 38 (5 May 1982).

Project Consult/Syndex. 2004. *Die Zukunft der europäischen Verteidigungsindustrie - Diskussionsgrundlage für die EMB-Konferenz in Brüssel,* 10 and 11 December, 2003. Frankfurt am Main.

Prössl, Christoph. 2018. "Waffenexporte: Bislang erst drei Kontrollen vor Ort" *Tagesschau,* 15 September, 2018.

Puetter, Uwe. 2012. "Europe's deliberative intergovernmentalism: the role of the Council and European Council in EU economic governance." *Journal of European Public Policy*: 161-178.

Quéau, Yannik. 2013. "Error 404: the European defence project you were looking for does not exist." *The Group for Research and Information on Peace and Security (GRIP). 04* December, 2013.

Rheinmetall Group. 2018. *Annual Report 2017.* https://ir.rheinmetall.com/websites/rheinmetall/English /3031/annual-reports.html

Rheinmetall Group. 2019. *Annual Report 2018.* https://ir.rheinmetall.com/websites/rheinmetall/English/ 2010/annual-figures.html

Rhodes, Chris, David Hough, and Louise Butcher. 2014. "House of Commons Library Privatisation. Research Paper 14/61". 20 November, 2014.

Rodrik, Dani. 2011. "The Globalization Paradox: Democracy and the Future of the World Economy." W. W. Norton & Company, 21 February, 2011.

RUAG. 2016. *Business activities in the UAE*. 08 December 2016. https://www.ruag.com/en/news/statement-ruag-regarding-business-activities-uaeruag-present-united-arab-emirates-over-20-years.

Schneider, Greg, and Renae Merle. 2004. "Reagan's Defense Buildup Bridged Military Eras." *Washington Post* 9 (2004): E1.

Schröder, Alwin. 2015."Deutsche Gewehre im Jemen: Bundesregierung verlangt Aufklärung von Saudi Arabien. "*Spiegel Online,* 20 June, 2015.

Schwer, Andreas. 2013. "Capital Markets Day 2013 Combat Systems - The largest one of three divisions." *Rheinmetall*, 08 November, 2013.

Spiegel Magazin. 1972. "Da tümmelt sich die Elite." DER SPIEGEL, Nr 28/1972.

Sprenger, Sebastian. 2018. "Tank maker takeover: Germany's Rheinmetall eyes acquisition of rival KMW." *Defense News*, 27 November, 2018.

State Department. 2016. "Blue Lantern End-Use Monitoring Program Office of Defense." Policy Directorate of Defense Trade Controls Bureau of Political-Military Affairs U.S. Department of State, October 30, 2016.

Stewart, Ian, and Nicolas Gillard. 2015. "Open Source and Trade Data for Non-Proliferation: Challenges and Opportunities" No. IAEA-CN-220.

Stockholm International Peace Research Institute. 2019. SIPRI Arms Transfers Database. https://www.sipri.org/databases/armstransfers.

Stockholm International Peace Research Institute. 2019. SIPRI Military Expenditure Database. https://www.sipri.org/databases/milex.

Vlachos-Dengler, Katia. 2004. *Off Track?*. RAND National Defense Research Institute.

War Weapons Control Act as last amended by Article 3 of the law of 11 October 2002, Federal Law Gazette I, p. 3970

Webb, Whitney. 2018. "US Provided `Intelligence and Bomb Used in Massacre of Yemeni Schoolchildren". Mint Press News. 13 August, 2018.

Wendt, Alexander. 1992. "Anarchy is what states make of it: the social construction of power politics." *International organization* Vol.46 no. 2 (Spring): 391-425.

Wendt, Alexander. 1999. *Social theory of international politics*. Cambridge University Press.

Whyte, Philip. 2007." Sarkonomics a user's guide." *Centre for European Reform*. 08 November, 2007.

Widman, Miriam. 2014." G3 Rifle Used by Militias Worldwide, Made in Germany." Handelsblatt, April 09, 2014. https://www.handelsblatt.com/today/politics/gun-exports-g3-rifle-used-by-militias-worldwide-made-in-germany/.

Wolf, K. (2015). *Putting numbers on capabilities: defence inflation vs. cost escalation.* European Union Institute for Security Studies.

Wolf, Martin. 2001. "Will the nation-state survive globalization." *Foreign Affairs*, *80*, 178.

Yemen and the global arms trade. DW Documentary. Deutsche Welle. 2018. https://www.dw.com/en/yemen-and-the-global-arms-trade/av-46580888.

Zeit Online. 2016. "Heckler und Koch will Waffenexporte erzwingen." *20* May, 2016. https://www.zeit.de/politik/ausland/2016-05/heckler-und-koch-waffen-exporte-ruestungs industrie.

Zeit Online. 2018. "Rheinmetall: Gabriel soll Waffenhersteller Rheinmetall geholfen haben." 06 March, 2018. https://www.zeit.de/politik/2018-03/rheinmetall-indien-sigmar-gabriel-korruptionsvorwuerfe.

Zeit Online. 2018."Rheinmetall- Rüstungsexporte nach Saudi-Arabien laufen indirekt weiter." *04* December, 2018. https://www.zeit.de/wirtschaft/unternehmen/2018-12/ruestungskonzern- rheinmetall-saudi-arabien-munitionslieferung-exportstopps-lieferungen

Annex I: Interview Overview

Code	Country	Position	Date
Ger-J-1	Germany	Journalist	12/06/2018
Ger-J-2	Germany	Journalist	16/06/2018
Ger-NGO-1	Germany	NGO Representative	23/07/2018
Ger-NGO-2	Germany	NGO Representative	01/08/2018
Ger-S-1	Germany	Scientist	13/06/2018
Ger-1-2	Germany	Scientist	10/01/2019
F-S-1	France	Scientist	08/2/2018
UK-NGO-1	UK	NGO Representative	13/07/2018
B-I-1	Belgium	Industry	10/07/2018
B-I-2	Belgium	Industry	15/07/2018
B-I-3	Belgium	Industry	23/07/2018
B-I-4	Belgium	Industry	27/07/2018
B-COARM-1	Belgium	COARM Representative	20/07/2018
B-EU-1	Belgium	EU Commission	30/07/2018
US-FO-1	USA	Foreign Office Official	20/10/2018
US-FO-2	USA	Foreign Office Official	25/10/2018
US-FO-3	USA	Foreign Office Official	03/11/2018
US-BW-1	USA	German Embassy	07/11/2018
US-BW-2	USA	German Embassy	08/11/2018
US-BW-3	USA	German Embassy	10/11/2018

Annex II: Practical example of Dual-Use licensing

To illustrate the workings of the regulation, imagine that a German firm that wants to export a computer (dual-use good) to a customer in the Middle East. First of all, it is the responsibility of the firm to identify the good it wants to export and as the firm wants to deliver outside the EU, Annex 1 of the Dual Use Regulation is applicable. After having browsed through the 240 pages of Annex 1, the good should be found in Category 4 named "computers" and it will be accompanied by a code, in this case for example 4A001 for notebooks[94]. Unlike in customs control lists where goods are codified according to the material they are made of[95], goods on the export list are classified according to technical product characteristics (based on the US Commercial Control List). This kind of classification goes a step further as it automatically indicates for which kinds of security issues a good may be relevant, such as national security, risk of WMD proliferation or terrorism.

Once the good has been identified as listed, the company must approach the national export office and apply for a license. In case of the German firm, they would apply to the Federal Office of Economics and Export Control (BAFA). Before that however, the firm is also required to analyse whether the good is listed on other relevant international regulations or directives, such as the EU Anti-Torture Regulation, the EU Regulation on Firearms and the EU Defence Equipment Directive. It is also important to verify that the exporting country is not subject to an embargo. If this is not the case and the good is not found on any of the EU regulation lists, it can still be listed on additional national lists. Each member state can have national special-items lists for dual-use goods, which is the case in Germany where specific dual-use items can be found on section B of the Export List[96]. Finally, if the customer is not located in a country that is subject to an embargo and the good is not listed on any export list, there is still a so-called `catch all clause´ that may force exporters to request a license. This provision can be found in Article 4 of the Regulation, and it allows national authorities to impose a licensing requirement for the export of items that are not listed but are or may be intended for:

- uses in connection with NBC weapons;

[94] Some countries have online search engines that help in the preparation of the license application. For instance, the UK government uses programmes called "Goods Checker" and "OGEL Checker"

[95] In Germany, customs control materials are codified by an 8-digit number

[96] Article 8 of the regulation allows Member States to have additional lists i.e. to impose a licensing requirement on items not listed in Annex I for "reasons of public security or human rights considerations" (9).

- a military end-use, if the purchasing or destination country is subject to an EU, OSCE or UN arms embargo; or
- for use as parts or components of military items listed in the national military list of the Member State that have been exported illegally.

If an exporter is aware that an item, software or service serves one of those purposes they must notify the authorities who can then decide to impose a licensing requirement. The catch-all instrument was used to be able keep export controls up to date with rapid technological developments and with new intelligence about possible military applications of civil items[97]. Therefore, Member States are supposed to report the use of the catch-all provision to other Member States and the Commission "where appropriate" so that additional goods can be listed if necessary. Only if the good is not listed on any national or European lists and the catch-all clause does apply, the good can be transferred without license requirement. In all other instances a company has to approach BAFA.

97 Between 2002 and 2007, the four main multilateral export control regimes all added similar catch-all clauses to their guidelines. The Wassenaar Arrangement in 2003, the Nuclear Suppliers Group in February 2006 and the Australia Group in June 2007.

Annex III: The EU Common Position Criteria

The Criteria of the EU Common Position on Arms Exports (without sub-clauses)

1. Respect for the international obligations and commitments of member states, in particular the sanctions adopted by the UNSC or the EU, agreements on non-proliferation and other subjects, as well as other international obligations.
2. Respect for human rights in the country of final destination as well as respect by that country of international humanitarian law.
3. Internal situation in the country of final destination, as a function of the existence of tensions or armed conflicts.
4. Preservation of regional peace, security and stability.
5. National security of member states and of territories whose external relations are the responsibility of a member state as well as that of friendly and allied countries.
6. Behaviour of the buyer country with regard to the international community, in particular its attitude to terrorism, the nature of its alliances and its respect for international law.
7. Existence of a risk that the military technology or equipment will be diverted within the buyer country or re-exported under undesirable conditions.
8. Compatibility of the exports of the military technology or equipment with the technical and economic capacity of the recipient country, taking into account the desirability that states should meet their legitimate security and defence needs with the least diversion of human and economic resources for armaments.

Source:

Council Common Position 2008/944/CFSP of 8 Dec. 2008 defining common rules governing control of exports of military technology and equipment, Official Journal of the European Union, L335, 8 Dec. 2008.

Annex IV: **Glossary**

Abbreviation	**Term**	**Definition**
ATT	Arms Trade Treaty	UN treaty that entered into force on 24 December 2014 and regulates the international trade in conventional weapons
AWG	Foreign Trade and Payments Act *(Außen-wirtschaftsgesetz)*	Law that regulates German foreign Trade
AW-Prax Journal	Practice in foreign trade Journal *(Außenwirtschaftliche Praxis)*	Export Journal for practitioners
AWV	Foreign Trade and Payments Ordinance (Außenwirtschaftsverordnung)	Ordinance that implements the AWG and further describes how foreign trade is regulated
BAE	BAE Systems PLC	British multinational defence, security and aerospace company. Its major customer is the US government
BAFA	Federal Office of Economics and Export Control *(Bundesamt für Wirtschaft und Ausfuhrkontrolle)*	German federal agency authorised to grant export licenses
BICC	Bonn International Centre for Conversion	German institute that researches disarmament and development issues

BITS	The Berlin Information-centre for Transatlantic Security	NGO providing expertise on military/security issues, especially in the field of disarmament
BMVg	The Federal Ministry of Defence	
BMWI	Ministry of Economy and Energy	
BSR	Federal Security Council (Bundessicherheitsrat)	Committee of the German Federal Cabinet that serves as a control and coordination body for security policy
BTWC	Biological and Toxin Weapons Convention	Convention on the Prohibition of the Development, Production and Stockpiling of Bacteriological and Toxin Weapons
CCFD- Terre solitaire		French NGO formerly the Catholic Committee against Hunger for Development
CDU/CSU	Christian Democratic Union/ Christian Social Union	Centre-right Christian democratic political alliance of two political parties in Germany
CETME	Centro de Estudios Técnicos de Materiales Especiales	Spanish government small arm design and development company
COARM	Working Party on Conventional Arms Export	EU Council working group concerned with export controls for conventional arms
COCOM	Coordinating Committee on Multilateral Export Controls	Former multilateral control body by the western bloc to control arms sales during the cold war

CFR	US Code of Federal Regulations	Rules and regulations by the executive departments and agencies of the US Government divided into 50 broad areas (titles)
CSFP	Common Foreign and Security Policy	The agreed foreign policy of the EU mainly for security and defence related purposes.
CWC	Chemical Weapons Convention	Arms control treaty that outlaws the production, stockpiling, and use of chemical weapons
DGA	The Direction générale de l'armement	French Government Defence procurement and technology agency
Diversification		Business strategy to add new products or services that are often unrelated to a company's portfolio (mostly) by acquiring other companies
EADS	European Aeronautic Defence and Space Company	Pre-2017 parent company of Airbus, now evolved into Airbus SE
EEAS	European External Action Service	Diplomatic service of the European Union
FDI	Foreign Direct Investment	Investment in the form of a controlling ownership in a business in one country by an entity or person based in another country
FDP	The Free Democratic Party	Centre/liberal political party in Germany.
FRG	Federal Republic of Germany	

GATT	The Gerneral Agreement on Tariffs and Trade	Preceded the WTO and was the major first multilateral measure to promote reduction of trade barriers
GIAT	Nexter Systems (formerly Groupement des Industries de l'Armée de Terre)	French armoured vehicle manufacturer, based in Roanne, Loire.
GKKE	Joint Conference Church & Development	Ecumenical work forum on development policy
GL	General Licenses	Multi-year flat-rate approvals for German military component deliveries
Golden Shares		A share in a company that gives control of at least 51 percent of the voting rights, especially when held by the government.
GTL	General Transfer Licences	Open licences, that allow a range of products to be transferred to specified recipients without requesting extra permission for each individual transfer
HADDEX	German Export Control Manual (Handbuch der deutschen Exportkontrolle)	Published by Bundesanzeiger Verlag, which publishes the official announcements of the Federal Government and the EU
HK	Heckler & Koch GmbH (HK)	*German* defence *company* manufacturing handguns, rifles, submachine guns etc.
ICT Directive	Directive on intra-EU-transfers of defence related products	Simplifies terms and conditions of transfers of defence-related products within the EU and EEA

	Directive 2009/43/EC	
ITAR	International Traffic in Arms Regulations	US regulatory regime to restrict and control the export of defence and military related technologies
KMW	Krauss-Maffei Wegmann GmbH & Co. KG	German Defence company producing armoured vehicles and Main battle tanks (MBT)
KNDS	The KMW+Nexter Defense Systems	European defence industry holding resulting from the joint venture between KMW and Nexter Systems
KWKG	War Weapons Control Act (Kriegswaffenkontrollgesetz)	Act Implementing Article 26 (2) of the Basic Law, regulates the manufacture, sale and transport of weapons of war
M&A	Merger and Acquisitions	Transactions in which the ownership of a company is transferred or consolidated with other entities
MBDA	MBDA	European developer and manufacturer of missiles (GER/F/I/UK)
MKEK	The Mechanical and Chemical Industry Corporation	Turkish Government-controlled group of military factories established in 1950
Monopsony		A market situation in which there is only one buyer, typically associated with the defence industry.

MoU	Memorandum of Understanding	Formal agreement between two or more parties, mostly governments
MRAP	Mine-Resistant Ambush Protected	United States military light tactical vehicles designed to withstand improvised explosive devices (IEDs)
MRCA	Multi-Role Combat Aircraft	Combat aircraft intended to perform a variety of roles in combat (Eurofighter Typhoon)
MS	European Union Member States	
MTCR	Missile Technology Control Regime	Multilateral export regime for the control of ballistic missiles
NBC Weapons	Nuclear, biological, or *chemical weapons*	
NETMA	NATO Eurofighter and Tornado Management Agency	Prime management body for the four-nation Typhoon programme.
Non- market Strategies		Business strategy to pursue strategic goals through political and social leverage e.g. corruption.
NPT	Non-Proliferation Treaty	International treaty to prevent the spread of nuclear weapons and promote cooperation in the peaceful uses of nuclear energy
NSG	Nuclear Suppliers Group	Export control regime to prevent nuclear proliferation by controlling the export of relevant materials, equipment and technology

RDM	Rheinmetall Denel Munition	Joint venture between formerly government owned Denel Ammunitions and Rheinmetall in South Africa
RMW Italia		Rheinmetall subsidiary involved in the production of ammunition and warheads
RUAG		Swiss aerospace and defence company
SALW	Small Arms and Light Weapons	
SAMI	Saudi Arabian Military Industries	State-owned defence company launched in 2017
Sarkonomics		Reference to French President Nicolas Sarkozy and his so-called *dirigiste* belief in an active role for the state in economic development (Whyte 2007)
SPD	The Social Democratic Party of Germany	The Social Democratic Party of Germany is a social-democratic political party in Germany.
TEU	*Treaty on European Union*	International treaties setting out the EU's constitutional basis
TFEU	Treaty on the Functioning of the European Union	Setting out the scope of the EU's authority to legislate and the principles of law in those areas where EU law operates.
UNCTAD	The United Nations Conference on Trade and Development	UNCTAD is the part of the United Nations Secretariat dealing with trade, investment and development issues.

UNSC	United Nations Security Council	One of the six principal UN bodies charged with the maintenance of international peace and security
Vertical integration		Business strategy of large companies to acquire smaller suppliers
WA	Wassenaar Arrangement	Successor of COCOM and first global arrangement on export controls for conventional weapons and sensitive dual-use goods

Zeitfracht Medien GmbH
Ferdinand-Jühlke-Straße 7
99095 Erfurt, Deutschland
produktsicherheit@kolibri360.de